MUTINY IN MY BODY

How running has saved my life.

Debbie Pentland
12/18/2012

It all began one autumn day.

<u>Saturday 22nd October 2011</u>

I awoke at 6.a.m. I had been looking forward to this day all year. `The Beachy Head Marathon` 26.2 miles of stunning scenery on the south coast around and through the Sussex countryside culminating in a wonderful downhill finish into Eastbourne.

The forecast was a good one. `Dry with occasional sunshine` Perfect! The last 2 years had been very wet, very cold and very windy.

The only problem was, I didn`t feel too good today. However as this was a run or walk event I decided that I would walk, take it easy and enjoy the day.

 Little did I know as I sat there enjoying my porridge that 2 days later I wouldn`t be able to climb my stairs or lift my arms and less than 2 weeks later two of my friends would be pushing me in a wheelchair into hospital for the start of a long and very frightening 6 week stay.

This would be my hardest `Marathon` of all with many `mountains` to overcome. Today's Beachy Head would be a walk in the park in comparison.

This is my story of all the `ups` and `downs` of my marathon back to fitness and health despite all the odds.

`People are like T Bags
You don`t know how strong they are
Until you put them in Hot Water`

`What Lies Behind us and what lies before us are Tiny Matters compared with
What Lies within us! `

Monday 24rth October

I had had a constant headache now for about 3 months. The doc couldn`t work out what was wrong, although I was convinced that it was a side effect from the medication I was taking for severe stomach pains, however my GP didn`t agree.

On my last check up with my Rheumatologist I had told him of these stomach pains I had been experiencing. He had suggested I ask my GP to request a `Gastro` investigation. I had and he said he would rather try some medication for gastric reflux. I told him I didn`t think it was reflux but he was adamant that it was. I had now been taking these drugs for 4 months which is why I was certain it was the drugs causing the headaches. The stomach pains had caused me to lose much sleep over these past months and it was beginning to tell on my overall health.

I didn`t feel good at all this morning. I struggled to get out of bed and felt very lethargic. However I had a Tai Chi class at 10.am, maybe I`ll feel better after I freshen up and have some breakfast? The Show must go on!

I really struggled to cycle the 2 ½ miles to the community centre where I teach and once I started the class I was finding that my body wasn`t doing what I was asking of it. I couldn`t raise my arms any higher than my waist and my legs felt as if they didn`t belong to me anymore. I talked the class through and couldn`t wait to get back home to bed.

About 200 yards into my journey I fell off my bike! What`s happening to me? This is bloody scary! Somehow I managed to get home and almost collapsed stepping in through the door.

I have had days like this before. I have lived with Auto Immune Disease for the past 20 years. Systemic Lupus Erythematosis, Raynauds and Mixed Connective Tissue Disease. However despite all of this I had managed through healthy diet and lifestyle to lead a fairly active life, teaching exercise. Tai Chi and Qi Gong, Falls Prevention, Exercise to music and specialized classes for the blind and for amputees, mainly in the over 50`s age group.

I was also a runner albeit a very slow one. I would clock up around 25 miles a week and take part in a race most Sundays along with my husband Bob. I also did the gym twice a week, yoga and I cycled everywhere.

Usually when I had the odd bad day a couple of days off would have me bouncing back.

I was to take two weeks off and I wasn`t bouncing. I was finding over the next few days that I couldn`t get up my stairs without pulling myself up with my arms, my legs felt like they were filled with lead and my arms would hardly move. I was also having trouble swallowing and was consequently losing weight. I felt like a `ragdoll`. I also felt that my breathing was impaired, it felt as if I wasn`t getting a full lung of air when I breathed in. This wasn`t normal! My Lupus must be going `haywire` this time. Had I been over doing it?

I rang Rheumatology and explained my situation and got an appointment right away with Dr W my Rheumatologist. I took a taxi and when I arrived at the hospital Dr W and another doctor were waiting for me. As I was telling them what had been happening to me over the past few day s Dr H walked in ` Ah Here`s the fittest lady in Portsmouth!` he said `Not today doc` I replied. I demonstrated my muscle weakness and my inability to get myself up from a chair, I told him I had taken some time off work but I wasn`t bouncing back as I usually do.

He sent me along to get blood tests. They filled so many test tubes even the phlebotomist hadn`t heard of one of the tests that had been requested and wasn't sure which colour tube to put it in. She had worked there 10 years! Then I was sent along to X ray where I had a chest x ray done, next a lung function test. And then back to see Dr W. `We`ll see what the tests show up. I think that your Lupus is having a major flare up and may require an infusion , that's a massive dose of steroid which we put in intravenously but we`ll wait and see what the tests show. We`ll call you as soon as we have the results, it will take a few days. ` I got another taxi home and got back into bed.

8thNov

When I awoke I felt absolutely terrible. By now I could hardly move, I had lost almost a stone in weight and I was having double vision. I thought a nice warm bath would perk me up. I struggled to get my legs over the side to get in and almost collapsed into the warm soothing water. I was now very concerned about what was happening to me. I had never felt this bad before. When I tried to get out of the bath I found that I couldn`t get myself up off my backside, my legs wouldn`t move. What the hell is going on here I thought? I eventually had to slither out over the side like a new born calf released from its mother's womb and I collapsed in a heap onto the bathroom floor. Somehow I managed to drag myself to the phone and rang the Rheumatology Emergency number. A voice I recognised came on the answer machine. `We`ll get back to you within 48 hours` `Colin it`s Debbie Pentland here. I`ve just collapsed in the bathroom` I almost sobbed down the line. 20 minutes later Colin rang me back. ` Debs get in here NOW! We`ve been trying to ring you. `

Colin and I knew each other well. He was the Rheumatology Matron and he had invited me on several occasions to do talks on exercise and its benefits to various patient groups. I had also taken some of my class members along to various medical conferences to do Tai Chi Demonstrations. He knew how fit I normally was and he sounded quite worried.

Just as I was about to call a taxi my doorbell rang and blessings of blessings there stood two of my running friends Gary and Helen. One look was enough I burst into tears and fell into Gary's arms. Half an hour later they were wheeling me into the hospital where Dr W had found me a bed on a ward. What is happening to me? How could this be happening to me? I'm usually so full of beans.

They got me settled into bed and everything was a bit of a blur. The bright lights were making my head ache worse and I just wanted to sleep and not wake up again. Maybe I would feel better after a good restful sleep? Maybe I was asleep and all this was some awful nightmare?

Oh No! The nightmare was about to begin and I would be very much awake.

9th Nov 2011

I had never been in hospital before and I found it all quite terrifying. I hadn`t slept much at all last night it was so noisy in here. The nurses were around every 4 hours to take my observations (blood pressure, temperature, pulse, oxygen levels and lung function) also the lights were so bright in the corridor and shone all night into our ward.

Breakfast arrived but I couldn`t eat my porridge, my appetite had gone and besides my facial muscles and my tongue were not working properly.

The doctors were around quite early to do some reflex and co-ordination tests and to test the strength of my muscles and vision.

My pulse was 63 which the doctors thought was fine but I knew that my normal pulse was 53 and it being up by 10 points was anything but `fine`. As I was fit I had been below average which is `70` for some years now this was worrying to me. Now if they had a patient who was pulse reading 80 instead of 70 they would be concerned. I tried to explain my anxiety.

I felt absolutely exhausted. The nurses had given me Tramadol at 3am to help me sleep. I have never in my life taken sleeping pills and they were making me feel very sick. My mouth was filling up with foamy saliva and as my throat muscles were not working I couldn`t swallow it. I tried to cough it up but couldn`t and I felt I was choking. I couldn`t breathe and I was making strange panicky noises when the nurses ran over, and threw an oxygen mask over my face. ` Deep breaths, deep breaths` they were saying as one of them pulled a chair up underneath me. I was very frightened at this point and I was taken back to bed and told to try and get some rest.

 The lights were so bright in the ward I felt as if I was in one of those old war movies, you know `We have ways of making you talk!`. I just lay back on my pillow, threw my dressing gown over my head and cried my eyes out.

A while later I realised that I must look awful, I certainly felt awful so I asked the nurses if they would help me have a shower?

The first 5 days in hospital these days you are given a big bottle of `Hibiscrub` A pink, not very pleasant smelling liquid soap, this is to help combat the `bugs` M.R.S.A and the like. It has no lather so you still feel dirty afterwards, but at least I felt fresher.

Bob came to see me after work. He looked worried but joked `Whose going to cook my dinner?

We had been together for 32 years and in that time had only had 2 nights apart. We were two halves of a whole so parting was very hard when he had to go.

Thursday 10th November.

This morning I couldn`t seem to swallow my tea so I dropped a piece of chocolate sponge in and spooned it up. It helped a bit.

A Physiotherapist came to see me this morning and she told me that she had been told all about me by a colleague Anita, a running mate of mine. She wanted to see what mobility I had left.

We tried a few squats, leg swings, knee lifts and shoulder rolls, all of which I was finding very difficult to do.

Doctor George a Neurologist then arrived to do some more muscle and co-ordination tests with me. Then a chap from the Respiratory Unit wheeled in a lung function testing kit to see how my breathing was.

Next I was taken in a wheelchair down to Neurology for an EMG (electromylogram). A quite painful test where I was stuck with needles in various parts of my body to which an electric current was shot through to stimulate my muscles.(Yes its' that old war time movie again). The computer reads the muscle response. I must admit I was glad when it was all over.

The Neurologist said he was testing for MG `Myasthenia Gravis`. My first thought was to the posters I had recently seen on our seafront while out running of these three faces who couldn`t smile. The caption had read `Put A Smile On Someone`s Face because They Cannot Smile for themselves` As someone who is always smiling that would be the worst thing for me to have.

I always finished my Tai Chi Classes with the words `Remember your Inner Smile, and If you see some Poor Soul out there without a smile, Give Them One Of Yours!`. So the thought of having to live with MG terrified the life out of me.

After the doc scrutinized the results he told me that it was not Myasthenia Gravis, but it was something to do with the message from my brain to my muscles. `Phew` not MG but hey if that's the good news? The doc was very compassionate and rather than have me wait for a porter he took me back to the ward himself. I think he felt sorry for me as I looked so defeated.

As soon as I got back to the ward (this was turning out to be a very busy morning) Dr B Neurology Consultant and Dr W came to tell me that they were trying to get me a bed in Wessex Neuro Southampton General. Dr B explained that they would be able to do much more sophisticated testing to get to the bottom of what was happening to me. Dr B had a very kind and caring manner about her and I felt in safe hands.

I couldn`t sleep again that night. I felt exhausted but my mind was whizzing, I had never been so scared in my entire life before and I had had a lot to deal with over the past 20 years. Living with Lupus is no easy task. I remember when I was first diagnosed with it. It was the autumn of 1991. Twenty one years ago.

Two weeks before on the 6th September I had been up in Aldershot doing an Army Assault Course.

Essentials Magazine had asked people to write in with a `challenge` idea. Well I had always wanted to do an Army Assault Course with one of those long zip wire thingy`s so I wrote to them.

The day arrived. I drove into the `PARA Regiment` car park. I was met by Major B who had the most gorgeous brown eyes and his P.R man a Capt. A. I then met the reporter from the magazine and the photographer, we all had a chat over coffee to explain what would happen. I was kitted out and driven by jeep to the course...

I looked on in horror when I saw that the whole assault course was about 15´ off the ground. . I should have suspected something like this by the fact that Essentials Magazine had chosen the Parachute Regiment Camp for our adventurous day out. However I had not given it much thought.

Ugh! What had I let myself in for? What is it the Chinese say, `Be Careful What You Wish for? The Major asked me if I'd been in training. `Well` I said `I do a lot of swimming, walking and cycling, but how do you train for a high wire act`

Next one of the 2 P.T.1`s that were to look after me for the day came over. `You won`t need this, ` off came my belt` or this`, off came my jacket, then my jumper. Crikey how far are we going to go here? I thought. He is cute but hey I`m a happily married woman. So there I was T shirt, khaki trousers, helmut and boots ready or as ready as I was going to be to give it my Best Shot. THE BODY WILL FOLLOW THE HEART AND MIND.

The other P.T.1 was going to lead the way `Just follow me `he says, hmmmm. Off we go. Well everything was going fine until I got to this bit where you have to jump from one 6" plank to another one which is about a foot lower and several inches apart. Doesn`t sound too bad you say. Not if the said planks were about a foot or two from the ground `no probs` but bear in mind these Buggers were 15´ up in the air. I looked down woh!!! Major Brown Eyes shouts up to me ` Come on we have kids of 15 and 16 at the weekends doing this. ` `Yes `, I said ` When I was that age I wouldn`t have hesitated either` I had grown up with 4 brothers and had always been a bit of a tomboy , up for anything, but hey I shouted back `I`ve grown up since then and with age comes FEAR!`

Oh Well `TRIUMPH IS JUST THE WORD TRY WITH A LITTLE BIT OF UMPH` Here goes and I launched myself at it, made it to the other side where the P.T.1. grabbed me to steady me I was shaking like a leaf and my poor heart was beating the retreat boom boom diddy boom boom. I wobbled like a weeble but I didn`t fall down. They all cheered me below. I managed a smile. What`s next? Bring it on! Phew.

The next obstacle was a mere 8foot wall Mmmmm. Being only 5`4" this wasn`t going to be easy. I made a stab at it three or four times grappling for the top as I ran at it and failing miserably. It was no good my arms just were not long enough. The P.T.1 got up on top the wall and said he would haul me up on the next launch I made. It worked! Now, how do I get down? I thought. I decided I would have to what we call in Scotland `dreep` it. I lowered myself over the wall held on with both hands to the top and then simply let go and dropped like a stone in a heap to the ground. I got up and made a dash to the finish and collapsed on my back, elated, grinning from ear to ear, and heart pounding and covered in sweat, not from the exertion but from sheer Terror.

I looked up to see 6 pairs of eyes smiling down at me. `Right ` Major Brown eyes says with his hands on his hips ` Not a bad effort but not a very good time, How about another couple of cracks at it?

Another couple of cracks at it! You`re having a laugh Mate! I`d survived a near death experience I wasn`t going to over play my hand! `Eh No Thanks and I won`t be joining the Parachute Regiment either`. Everybody laughed.

As we drove back to base for a welcome hot bath the Major asks what made me want to do this. Well I told him I set myself a challenge every year a kind of `Bucket List` if you like. You know things I want to do before I kick the bucket. `Ah Next year you could come up here and do a parachute jump with us? ` To which I grinned and said `Done one, A few years ago for Oxfam`. `How did that go? ` He asked me. I told him the story. It was in the summer of 1986.

It was a 2,000 feet jump with a mushroom parachute. There were 3 of us jumpers in the plane, (a wee 4 seater Cessna with the seats removed) along with the instructor and the pilot. Our parachutes weighed 4 ½ stone so walking to the plane from the jeep had been hard work. The emergency chute which was attached to my belly and the main chute on my back weighed me down so much I could hardly move. We all waddled to the plane and crawled in to position ourselves on the floor. The pilot took us up to 2,000 feet and hovered over the drop zone. We were ready to go. The door had been removed and I was the first up. `In the door `the instructor shouts over the noise of the engine. I shuffled on my backside into the doorway. `Go` I lean towards the open space and I'm off. The main chute is attached to the inside of the plane and should open in the time it takes to say `one thousand, two thousand, three thousand` we were then trained to` check canopy` if it hadn't opened then we were to curl over and pull the emergency cord of the belly chute. Well as soon as I left the plane all I could scream was `Shiiiiiiiiiiiiiiiiiittttttttt!!!!!!!! Next thing I knew the mushroom had opened and I felt a surge upwards. I reached up for my toggles which would control the parachutes direction. This is INCREDIBLE, WOH! , AWESOME.....
While I was enjoying the view not a care in the world I suddenly hear my ground instructor on the radio which is attached to my chute strap `Debbie Pull the left toggle` Well that's easier said than done. You need arms like Arnie Swarzanegger to pull these buggers. I pulled, nothing happened. `Deb, Pull your left toggle` `I'm pulling I'm pulling! ` I shout back, of course he couldn't hear me it was a one way radio. `Deb` He was getting excitable now `Deb, you f****** pull your left toggle or I'm gonna f****** well kick your ass when you get down here, you're heading for the f****** motorway. That did it. I didn't mind a kicked ass but I didn't fancy doing a James Bond landing on top of a lorry or worse still landing in front of one. A strength I didn't know I had allowed me to finally pull that toggle and I glided to safety heading for the big red square landing spot that was marked out in the stubble crop field. Phew. That was close I thought. I had glided in like a majestic swan landing on a smooth lake. I remembered to bend my knees and fall to one side on landing as we had been taught. I was elated. Wow, what a buzz. Then I quickly remembered I had to get up and run around the chute to stop it filling with air and dragging me through the rough field. I folded the chute in a figure of eight around my arms as we'd been shown. It didn't feel heavy at all now. In fact light as a feather. I was having an Endorphin (body's natural pain killer) rush. I couldn't feel any other emotion than Pure Joy!

Tears streamed down my cheeks and a smile from ear to ear covered my face. I walked back to the jeep for a hug from

Bob, the instructors and the other folks who had done their jumps earlier.

It had been a fabulous day and we had all raised a lot of money for Oxfam.

`Who Dares Wins`

Friday 11th November

I didn`t sleep much again last night. It was now quite a few days where I had lost sleep and it was beginning to show. My head was throbbing, my entire being was aching and I felt like I was wearing a suit of chainmail, my body felt so heavy.

I tried a few gentle exercises, squats, arm circles, stretches and a very short walk along the corridor trying to release those magical endorphins. It worked, I felt a little better. As I was walking back to bed the little old lady in the bed opposite me told me she was impressed with my workout. I went over pulled up a chair to have a wee chat with her. She told me that she had done exercise all her life and eaten healthily too. I must admit she did look very good for her age when she told me how old she was. We spent a couple of hours laughing and swapping stories. After a while the talking was becoming very difficult for me. My jaw seemed to stiffen up and it felt as if my tongue had doubled in size. I was also producing a lot of the foamy saliva again and my ears felt as if I had ear plugs in them. I went back to my bed for a rest.

The doctors came to see how I was and told me they are still waiting for a bed in Southampton Neuro.

Couldn`t eat lunch. Didn`t feel hungry anyway, but would have loved a cup of tea and something nice with it if I was able to swallow.

Veronica my masseuse who I normally see every 4 weeks for a full body massage appeared just after lunchtime. She had brought me a lovely bunch of flowers, she had also very thoughtfully brought her aromatherapy massage oils and a couple of hand towels to give me a face, neck and shoulder massage. The ward smelled gorgeous with the scent of rosemary and Lavender and LLang LLang. As I sat there looking out of the window enjoying Veronicas healing hands on my neck and shoulders the other 5 ladies in the ward were all saying `I`m next please` in hopeful jovial voices.

Gary and Helen and another running friend Julia all arrived, and then Stan my friend from my Tai Chi class (who also brought me flowers) appeared next. As they all gathered around my bed for a cheery chat I tried to look cheerful. I didn't want them to see just how worried I was.

Alas you`re not allowed flowers in hospitals these days. So I gave Veronica`s flowers to a lovely lady in the bed next to me who was going home today. I`ve never seen a face light up like hers did. She had been telling me earlier that she was so pleased to be going home as she was a carer for her son and she had been so worried about him. I don`t think she had had flowers given to her in a long time and it did my heart good to know that she appreciated the gift so.

I gave Stan's flowers to Veronica for giving me such a wonderful massage.

As I sat listening to all the news from my friends Dr B and Dr W appeared`. Good news. We`ve got you a bed in Neuro` The transport would be here shortly, so my friends helped me to pack up the few belongings I had with me.

My weight was now 8st 10lb my head ached despite the joy my friends had brought me and I felt awful. An hour later, my friends had all gone, two ambulance men came to take me on to the next and most frightening part of my journey.

We went out through the `Departure Lounge` Yes, I know. It was just like they have in the airports. I half expected there to be a duty free shop. I was checked out at the desk and wheeled out into the cool night air in a wheelchair. The ambulance men were very nice and helped me onto a stretcher in the ambulance tucked a nice thick quilt over me and strapped me in telling me that the journey at this time of night would take about 1 ½ hours so to try and get some rest, there would be no siren so it should be quiet for me. I lay there with all kinds of awful thoughts going through my mind.

When we finally arrived I was wheeled in through the main entrance to what looked like Cascades Shopping Centre. I thought I was hallucinating! I was a little bit drugged up with a morphine shot the nurses had given me to help with the pain just before I left Portsmouth. But I thought I'm not that drunk? `What am I doing in Cascades? ` I asked. `You`re in Southampton General` they replied. Then I spied it. I must be hallucinating? `Burger King!! Burger King? In a hospital you must be seeing things Deb `What the hell is Burger King doing in a hospital? ` I asked the ambulance guys. They were shaking their heads also in disbelief and agreed it was crazy. `Incredible isn`t it and they wonder why people don`t get well when they are allowing them to eat that junk` Good God I thought.

Before I left Q.A I had asked the nurses to let Bob know that I had been transferred. Bob told me later this is how that conversation went.

Nurse: Hello Mr Pentland Its Queen Alexandra Hospital here. Just to let you know your wife has been transferred to Wessex Neuro Southampton.

Bob: Could you give me the ward name and the phone no please?

Nurse: She is in Stanley Graveson Ward.

Bob: Could you spell that please?

Nurse: S.t.a.n.l.e.y. then Grave as in when you die...son.

Bob: (silence)   Poor Bob, as if he wasn`t worried enough his face must`ve been a picture. We laugh about it now and it`s been a funny story to tell our friends and family but at the time. What on earth was that nurse thinking? Or I guess she just wasn`t thinking eh. Ha-ha.

Well once onto the ward I was put to bed and given a sleeping pill and some codeine for the pain. I`d had more drugs in the past 4 days than I'd had in 14 years. I was just dropping off when I hear knock knock and my curtain opened. A head appeared through the gap. There stood the most gorgeous guy I'd seen in a long time `Can I come in? ` He asks. Can you come in, I'm dead but I'm not that dead I thought. `Sure` I replied. In walked this handsome specimen in blue scrubs. I think my pulse rate went right up there and then. I thought I'm dreaming, I must be dreaming, either that or I've died and gone to heaven? `I'm the night duty doctor on tonight is it ok if I examine you? You carry on I thought take your time. He did a few tests just like the ones I'd had done at Q.A then smiled and told me to try and get some rest, the doctors would all be around in the morning to see me and that someone would get to the bottom of it and try not to worry. He left and I never did see him again all the time I was at Southampton. Maybe I had been dreaming after all?

Actually, I did check a couple of weeks later who he was and yes he was real, he was one of the surgeons who had just happened to be on duty the night I came in. Lucky me.

Saturday 12th November

I was getting really frightened now. There's some scary looking things going on in this ward. By now I could hardly move and I needed to be wheeled to the bathroom by the nurses. I was in the High Observation Ward right next to the nurse's station so, they told me, they could keep an eye on me. I was also the only female here. The other 3 patients were all men. What made matters even worse was that I couldn't talk to any of them. One, I guessed had dementia, another was always asleep and the third chap was a pretty scary looking big chap with a thick black beard and he wore a soft helmet on his head to protect him when he fitted. This fella would wander up to the foot of my bed and stand there staring at me until one of the nurses would come to take him back to bed. He really did frighten me.

My head was now too heavy to hold up so when I sat in bed it just hung helplessly to one side. I had to prop it up on a pile of pillows. My legs felt like they were made of jelly and my arms felt like they were filled with lead.

The nurses wheeled me into the bathroom to give me a shower and wash my hair. The `Hibiscrub` was out again. How embarrassing to be sat there naked and have to be washed all over by a complete stranger. I know for a nurse it's nothing, but for the patients, especially the first time, it's a feeling I wouldn't wish on anyone.

I was being monitored for `obs` every 4 hours. This would become a regular routine for me along with the dreaded stomach injection to stop `DVT ` blood clotting in the legs. The injection felt just like a bee sting, which was a particular delight to endure and left a wee bruise where the skin was punctured. I wondered what picture I would get if I joined up the dots?

Sunday 13th November

`When was the last time you opened your bowels? 'Or `Have you opened your bowels today? 'was to become the morning greeting from the nursing staff and to make matters worse, you would then be shown a chart presuming of course you answered yes with delightful pictures known as the `Bristol Stool Chart'. This had a coloured picture of every conceivable variation and to be honest some of them didn't look human. I wondered if maybe they'd got hold of a veterinary's chart instead. It certainly cheered everyone up on the ward and gave us all a laugh in a pretty miserable situation.

I couldn't eat anything today. I was still awake at 2.am and really scared. What's happening to me?

My monthly's decided to start tonight to add to my misery. They had caught me out as I had lost all track of time since being in hospital and of course I had no tampons with me. Luckily the nurses came to the rescue and told me they could provide some. Actually what they could provide was `nappy pads` yes girls you all remember them I'm sure, those muckle pads that stick to the inside of your pants and make you walk like Mick Jagger. I hadn`t worn those since I started my periods at age 13. Also the snag was that I didn`t have any pants with me either. So once again the nurses had a solution to my problem. They produced what I can only describe as a cut off pair of extremely thin see through white tights. So there I was with my sexy underwear filled with a chunky nappy and walking like Mick. Just wait till Bob sees these. Heehee

Bob is a Postman. He`s up really early and does a very active delivery and also has a 10 mile round trip cycling to work. To visit me here in Southampton involves a cycle, a train then a bus all of which take about 2 ½ hours each way. So I told him only to visit 2 or 3 times a week. I didn`t want him getting run down. Besides he was also dealing with all the phone calls from family in Scotland and friends and there had been a lot of calls. He was very worried and it showed in his lovely face.

When he arrived he put me into a wheelchair to take me outside for some fresh air. We are both outdoor people and I had really been missing the outside world.

As he pushed me around in the chair I could hardly sit upright I had the most tremendous feeling of Doom come over me! Was this to be our life from now on? I wondered if my life would be that of an invalid with Bob having to do everything for me. Weeks later when I was finally out of hospital Bob shared the fact that he had felt the same that day.

When he left that night for home I cried into my pillow. Later that evening I tried to take my painkillers with some water and they got stuck in my throat. I couldn`t breathe. I was choking making those strange noises again. The nurses ran over with the oxygen mask, threw it over my face and once again I heard `Deep breathes Deep breathes`. Oh My God! Am I going to die in here?

When I recovered I couldn`t stop crying I was so distraught. What is happening to me?

The doctors were coming around every hour now to check up on me I guess they were worried too. I had to do a lung function test each time, I think they thought my lungs were about to pack up.

Monday 14th November.

 Today I was feeling absolutely shattered. My head was throbbing, I couldn`t eat anything as I was unable to chew or swallow and anyway I had no appetite.

The physiotherapist came to test my strength, it was zero. Doctors came to do some more tests on my muscles and my vision.

Dr S came to test my strength. I was getting weaker if that was possible. He said he wanted to do a muscle biopsy which he would take from my thigh. He said that they all suspected my problem was a malfunction where the message from the nerve was unable to connect to the muscle to stimulate it. By doing the core biopsy they hoped they could come up with some answers and get a diagnosis. He explained what he was about to do.

First he would inject an anaesthetic into my thigh, and then he would drive a needle deep into my thigh muscle like a skewer and pull out a core sample.   Mmmmmm......... sounds wonderful I thought. `O.K. ` I said `when?` to which he replied `Now` oh , no time to prepare myself then, well maybe just as well, no time to ponder over it either. The doc told me he would talk me through the whole procedure as he went along.

I kept my eyes closed the whole time (I hate needles) When he put the needle in to take the sample I didn`t expect what happened next? Wham! I felt as if I'd been pinned to the bed by an arrow shot from a crossbow! The needle felt like it had gone right through my leg and out the other side, I almost shot up to the ceiling! Well I certainly hope he gets some answers from this one because he told me if he did not then a further biopsy would be required and that he would take that from my ankle. Good God! I hope not. He then showed me the piece of my muscle he had removed before stuffing it into a test tube. It looked just like a tiny piece of raw meat, which I suppose it was.

I had to have sleeping pills again tonight. I wish I could get rid of this awful headache and get a proper night's sleep. I thought `This is not my life `.

Tuesday 15th November.

I`ve been in hospital one week now but it feels like a month. I feel really depressed and anxious. I had always felt that with my Lupus and all the other things I have wrong with me that I would never make `old age` I was O.K. with that. The thought of having to work so hard to stay well for many years to come would finally take its toll on me, but hey at 52 I`m too young to die.

I was showered by the nurses again. It is really frustrating having to wait until someone is free to take me in and give me a shower. Then being wheeled into the wet room helped onto the shower seat and washed while I sat there helpless, unable to move my arms, my head lolling to one side as my muscles couldn`t hold it upright. Even my speech was becoming slurred I sounded as if I was drunk. It`s a very long time since I was drunk I might add but I still remember how it felt. The nurse dried me and combed my hair. She then dressed me as I could do none of this myself now. Next I sat on the chair by the sink rested my arm on the side of the sink so I could brush my teeth, I could hardly move the toothbrush but somehow I managed. At least I felt fresh and clean.

After the shower I went to have a pee and I felt that although I felt desperate to go I could not. I told the nurse and she told me to try running a tap to see if that would help. I did and it helped a little but I still felt like I was not emptying my bladder. Oh God! Now my water works were shutting down Great! I thought what have I done to deserve all this? Was I a really nasty person in a previous life? It can`t be this life. I had always tried to do good things and I always treated others as I`d like to be treated myself. I had inherited a really caring nature from my mum. She was always doing nice things for others and bringing happiness wherever she could. I had always tried to follow her example. So why is all this happening to me? `This is not my life`

The Physiotherapists popped in again. They told me they have been told that I must rest for now. I couldn`t do anything else the way I feel at the moment.

My next visitor was the Speech and language Therapist or (s.a.l.t.) as they are known. She was very nice and said she had come to assess my swallowing. She produced a tray with a pot of yogurt, a glass of water a pot of cold ambrosia custard and a thick strawberry mousse on it. I thought we were about to play a game.

First though she put a stethoscope to my neck` mmmmmmm not much happening there ` she said. She then proceeded to spoon feed me tiny amounts of the yogurt while simultaneously listening to my throat through her stethoscope. This procedure was repeated with the other items on the tray. I was then spoon fed tiny teaspoonful`s of water which I struggled to get down. It was obvious to us both that my swallow had packed up. However she then produced a tub of granules which she added to the water which turned the water in to what looked to me like wall paper paste. Good God, does she expect me to swallow that? She tried, It was not going anywhere either.

`I think we will try a puree diet dinner tonight. Failing that then I`m afraid we`ll have to put in a Naso gastro tube for now and feed you through your nose. All your drugs will have to be crushed up mixed with water and put up the tube as well as your water. Don`t worry it`s just until you get your swallow back` she said smiling at me. I think she could see how frightened I looked at the prospect of that.

Well that evening, Dinner arrived. I must admit to a bit of anticipation. At last something I might be able to eat. The nurse placed the covered plate in front of me. I could hear the other patients all oohing and aahhing at their meals. The food was very good in here. I lifted the steaming lid from my plate. What I saw looked like something I had often stepped in while out on a cross country run! It was what I can only describe as a `cowpat` and it smelt like one too! I could feel the bile rising. I quickly put the lid back on before I started to imagine a big footprint in it. It really did look disgusting. `There is No Way I am going to eat that` I said to the nurse who was hovering nearby. ` Let`s put the NG tube in ` I said. She had that look on her face that told me she didn`t blame me, she wouldn`t eat it either. She had obviously seen people's reaction to this muck before.

I did manage a small cup of apple puree but it took me 25 minutes to eat it on the end of a teaspoon. It was such an effort for so little gain.

<u>Wednesday 16th November.</u>

A team of 5 doctors came around early to say that` It's not Cancer but still don`t know what it is yet` They still think it is a nerve/muscle problem. NOT CANCER! Bloody Hell I didn`t even know they suspected that. As for it being a nerve/muscle problem. Well I could tell you that, I can hardly move here. I am lying in bed unable to sit upright, shuffle up or down or sideways, roll over. I can hardly move my legs and my arms are useless. I still have a little bit of grip in my hands however so I can grab hold of the side panels of my bed to manoeuvre myself enough to get semi-comfortable. The power though is just not there. It is like trying to move a dead weight. My ankles I can point and flex. So it appeared that the only parts of me that were working were my extremities, my feet and hands. Everything else was shutting down or had shut down. My ears, nose and throat, eyes, breathing, bladder function, all major muscles voluntary and involuntary were failing me.

The tears started to flood down my cheeks. I couldn`t lift my arms up to wipe away the tears. I looked up at the doctors and looked at Dr S. `Am I dying? ` I sobbed. Dr S came around to the side of my bed knelt down beside me and took my hand in his two warm hands. He looked into my eyes and gently smiling said in a soft voice `No you are not going to die. We will find out what is wrong with you but it may take a little time. `

What worried me now though was that I might not die but that I would always now be like this. A `Ragdoll 'and that I would have to live the rest of my life like this!

`A Man Who Fears Suffering is Already Suffering What He Fears`

The doctors did a few more tests. Can you poke your tongue out? Move it side to side? Poke your tongue into your cheek? Touch your top, bottom lip? Can you whistle? I tried them all I couldn`t do any. That's weird I told them all I was normally a very good whistler. I could whistle like a navvy. In fact I often whistled to get attention in my exercise classes. It always brought about a grinning silence.

Next the doctor asked me to pull him towards me and push him away. I wasn`t too bad at the pull to but hopeless at the push I just had no power. Let`s hope that muscle biopsy shows up some clue.

After the doctors all left the nurse could see how scared I was and she came over to me sat on my bed and took my hand in hers. `Do you know they call this the Sherlock Holmes Ward? All the doctors with patients with puzzling conditions send their conundrums to us and our team of excellent doctors all put their heads together and always come up with an answer, but sometimes it takes a bit of time. You are in the best place here, they will find out what it is that's wrong with you. Try not to worry and try and get some rest.

They were all very kind in here. As many of us were light sensitive they had been turning the ward lights off during the day and only putting the big lights on during drug rounds in the evening. We all had our own bedside lamps for reading which made for a much cosier atmosphere and also made getting some rest much easier.

It was autumn time. This was my absolute favourite time of year. I love to hear the leaves rustling in the breeze and especially love to run through a forest on a blustery day. The sounds of the leaves crunching beneath my feet, I am like a kid in a sand pit. It is the best kind of music to my ears. I adore the colours of autumn. The reds, the gold's, browns and yellows as the trees changing colour are a delight to the eyes. I particularly love the smell of a bonfire. I also love digging out a pumpkin and lighting it and placing it in a prominent position to bring a smile to the face of any passer-by. The flocks of geese gaggling as they fly overhead in massive flocks coming in for the winter are all annual delights that I really look forward to each year. However being stuck in here I would miss it all. There was a very small saving grace. If I looked out from the neighbouring ward window into the quad that was the outdoor seating for the café in the hospital there was one lone tree and a few shrubs. I had been dragging myself over there to feast my eyes on that solitary tree every day and watched as each day more and more leaves were turning their autumn colours and then beginning to form a colourful carpet beneath its boughs. How I wished I could go out there and stomp around to feel and hear those crisp leaves scrunch beneath my feet. Oh I missed my outdoors and fresh air.

As each day elapsed and my tree began to look bare I was reminded of a film I had seen years ago. I can't remember anything about the film apart from the fact that a lady was lying in a hospital bed watching a tree outside her window with its leaves all moulting in the autumnal weather. She had decided that when the last leaf would fall that is when her life would end she would cease to exist along with the shedding of the tree's last leaf so too would she take her last breathe.

 Well she didn't die, because one lone leaf remained stubbornly clinging to the branch. It turned out that someone had painted that last leaf there. I wish I could remember more about that film as I now hoped that someone had painted one leaf to my tree. I didn't want to die in here.

Just after I had got back to bed the chaplain appeared. That put the frighteners on me I can tell you. Has he come to read me my last rights? Does he know something that I don't? Was that a measuring tape he had hanging out of his pocket or just his rosary beads? I relaxed when he cheerily says `Just doing the rounds` Phew!!!! Thank God for that. Just as well I`ve got a good sense of humour. It certainly helps in here.

I always try to look on the bright side of everything. Did you know you can learn a lot in hospital? I will give you an example. Who are these morons who create designs for certain equipment that goes into hospitals? They have obviously no idea what it is like to be a patient. What am I talking about folks? The Loo`s.

Who needs to have a physiotherapy session when you get all the exercise you need just trying to go for a pee. Yes, you all nod your heads, you know what I'm about to say don`t you?

First there is the flush button you have to push into the wall, which is all very well if you`ve got fingers as strong as Mr Universe. Then there is a particular favourite of mine. `The loo roll game` A massive roll of paper sits sealed inside a capsule placed on the wall behind you so far back that you`d need to be a contortionist to extract a piece. You can fiddle and twiddle for ages trying to first find the end, second grab the end and pull and thirdly get an adequate supply. As I couldn`t hold up my arm I had to hold one arm by the other which was balanced on my now so skinny thigh. It was exhausting.

I seem to remember Billy Connelly doing a sketch on this very theme. It was making me chuckle just thinking about it.

It took a while but I finally got it sussed! Where there`s a will there`s a way. Get the paper out before you sit down. I would like to get my hands on those designers though. However my workout would not be over until I had levered myself up off the seat. When you have no muscle power it is as if your brain is sending messages to a mere bag of bones. It gave me a real insight into the problems that the older generation I teach in my `Falls Prevention` classes have to combat on a daily basis and reiterated the importance of keeping your muscles strong with regular functional exercise.

Two of the exercises I teach in these classes are how to get up from the chair without using your hands and how to get up from the floor by yourself. What was really scaring me now was that I had been teaching this stuff for years and now I couldn`t do it myself.

Will I ever be able to work again? Will I have to live on Disability allowance for the rest of my life? Mmmm.

My mouth is now producing massive amounts of saliva and as I cannot swallow or spit it out I have to resort to the suction tube by my bed. It is just like the ones at the dentist.

Thursday 17th November

Now it was established that I was unable to swallow anything, I was to be fitted with a nasogastric tube. The thought didn`t thrill me at all!

Dr Ash, one of the Neuro- surgeons and a nurse were to do the procedure. I was terrified, I can tell you and I can honestly say it was the worst thing I have had to go through in my entire life.

I was propped up in bed with pillows either side. The doc sat on one side the nurse on the other. The nurse held my hand the whole way through and stroked my hand to try to comfort me. The tube has a wire running through it to make it easier to feed up through the nostril and then the worst part of all is up and over the bridge of the nose. `Keep swallowing, it helps it down` the doc kept saying. I cannot describe how uncomfortable it was. It was bringing tears to my eyes and a sweat over my entire body. My prison issue pyjamas were soaked and sticking to my back. I was in that war movie again being tortured.

A few weeks ago I had had a Gastro-investigation which meant having a surgical team send a `camera down my throat into my stomach` and biopsy`s taken from my stomach lining. It was an awful experience but it was nothing compared to what I was going through now.

The nurse was telling me how well I was doing, probably because I wasn`t yanking the damn thing back out. It was alright for her to sit there, had she ever had one put in? They should all go through the experience so they can feel empathy with the patient. It should be compulsory in their training. They would then be able to talk you through reassuringly from experience. If she had told me that once it was up over the bridge of my nose it would be plain sailing from then on in it would`ve helped and saved me a lot of anguish. Weeks from now I would have my 4th NG tube inserted by a nurse who had asked in training to try it. She was fantastic. Her approach was `Right then we will have this in in a jiffy. Once it`s up over the bridge we`re in, so bear with it Deb and it`ll soon be over`

Eventually it was in. It felt so uncomfortable I thought I would never get used to it. At least I could now get some food and water inside me.

That afternoon Steve and Julie two of my running friends came to visit. Poor Jules was very upset at the sight of me I could see that she was holding back the tears. The only time I see these two is when we are at running events together all glowing with health. Now here I was looking so ill, propped up in bed hardly able to move. I couldn`t even lift my arms up to give them both a hug and of course my new` Bling` the NG tube must`ve looked very scary.

Later that afternoon after my friends had gone I was wheeled down by a porter to Neuro- Science on B level for tests.

Two guys introduced themselves and explained that they were going to do multiple tests on my arm and leg muscles and possibly my facial muscles too. They apologised in advance that the tests would be quite painful but hopefully they would be able to come up with a diagnosis. Dr D one of the doctors who had been looking after me came in. He said this was the field he was very interested in and could he watch.

So there I was sat upright against a backrest on the examination table. The lights in the room were very bright and it was extremely warm. They stuck needles into my arms and legs and they were wired into a computer and screen. An electric current was then shot through me stimulating my muscles to work thus making my limbs shoot up in the air. It was very painful and I was trying not to cry. The results were showing up on the screen like a graph. They seemed very interested in the results as they all gathered around the screen. To me the picture looked like the profile of a hilly run. Just like the sort of thing that comes with your race information pack. I wished it was a run profile I was looking at.

I had been in that room for 2 ¼ hours. It was now 6.15pm. I was exhausted. I was also covered in sweat from head to toe; even my hair was sticking to my head. It was definitely a bad hair day. It was not just because it had been so hot in there but it was from the sheer terror of the whole experience. It had all been so painful. Then what would they find? Once again torture! That war movie again.

I was quite willing to go through the trauma if it would provide some answers. The worst fear is the unknown. Once I knew what it was I could start to fight back.

`This is not my life`

Afterwards the Neuro boys were finished with me I was wheeled out into the corridor to await a porter to take me back to my ward. I was very anxious to get up there as Bob said he would be coming at 6pm. I was looking forward to seeing him so much.

The feeling of uselessness as I sat there frustrated at the fact that I could not get myself to the lift and had to rely on others was overwhelming. Tears started to roll down my cheeks.

Finally someone came and I was wheeled back to my ward. There stood Bob and all I could do was burst into tears and fall into his arms. I badly needed a hug. As he wrapped his arms around me I so wanted to reciprocate but these useless limbs of mine would not oblige.

I must have looked a sight. All hot and sweaty and face red and swollen with crying but Bob smiled and held me close. I lay down on my bed and Bob pulled the curtain around for a bit of privacy. He then got onto the bed behind me and we lay like spoons in a drawer as he snuggled me up and the warmth from his body seeped into mine. Then he asked me what I had been up to.

I managed to get the whole story out through the sobbing. I actually found myself saying my goodbyes to him. I really did not feel that I was going to live much longer. I told him that he must find someone to love and care for and someone who could care for him. I tried to make light of it by saying that I would come back and haunt him until he found someone. I joked that he had better make sure she was a runner. Of course he mumbled the usual responses to my ramblings but hugged me all the tighter.

My tears were adding to my already damp pyjamas and my heart was heavy. I didn't want Bob to go. I wished he could stay with me as I had this overwhelming feeling that I would not see him again.

After he left I sobbed into my pillow.

It was many weeks later that Bob told me that after leaving the hospital that night he had sunk down onto a bench outside in the dark, put his head in his hands and cried his heart out. In 32 years together I have never seen him cry or even come close.

He missed his bus to the station but was lucky enough to hop on the next one which just got him there in time as his train was about to leave.

I couldn't sleep that night. I had all these awful thoughts going through my head. Who would look after my Bob? How would my family in Scotland take it? I hadn't even told any of them I was in here as I didn't want them to worry. They all lived so far away. I was thinking of all my friends I would miss and of all the good times I'd had in my life and all the things I still wanted to do and see.

I hadn't ticked off all of my `Bucket List` yet.

Friday 18th Nov

08.40am.A group of 4 doctors appeared around my bed all looking very serious.

Dr S said that the muscle tests I had endured last night had confirmed that I had LEMS. Lambert Eaton Myasthenic Syndrome.

Before he could get anymore out I broke down in tears. I wanted to wipe them away but my arms were useless so they just ran down my face in torrents. Dr S quickly came around to the side of my bed hunkered down and took my hand in both of his and proceeded to tell me more.

LEMS is extremely rare about 1 in 2 million in the U.K he said in a gentle voice that the reason they had not thought of it was because it usually affects men and is usually found in people who smoke so I did not fit the profile. His next words filled me with the first sign of hope I'd had since I came in. `It is treatable` It was tears of relief now that streamed down my face. He went on to tell me that the drug treatment was very expensive but not to worry they would get me on it today. He said that I would get back to normal but it would take time. How much time he couldn't say. The problem was with LEMS being so rare they just did not know.

To think just a few hours ago I had thought that my only way out of here was in a box!

I asked if I would be able to run again. They all looked at each other with a gloomy expression on their faces. `Let's take it one step at a time` Little did I realise then that he meant that literally. Then another bombshell exploded. `From what we understand, exercise usually makes the condition worse` and then another bombshell dropped `Most patients with LEMS will have an underlying cancer...` That hit me like a brick to the head. Cancer oh my God! That would mean Chemotherapy. How would my poor body with all that I have wrong with me cope with that awful stuff? I gloomily thought, I was a gonna one way or another.

I was booked in for 4 scans. The doctor told me I would need to have a chest ultrasound, then a chest and lung x ray, C.T. scan and a P.E.T scan. Dr B my consultant then joined us to prescribe my drug therapy.

Firstly I was to have IV/IG a five day intravenous drip through a cannula in my arm. Intravenous Immunoglobulin is a blood product drawn from the plasma of 1,000 donors. Wow! It contains special proteins which belong to a class of immunoglobulin's also called antibodies.

Antibodies are normally produced by our own immune system and help fight infection. Auto Immunity means that my own antibodies are fighting against me instead of for me. Turncoats as it were. (Mutiny in my body) So by having IV/IG I was in effect recruiting an army of 1,000 fighters from Donors (Thank you all) to help me win my battle. Great I thought. I had a vision of Blue painted faces dressed in kilts. `You`ll Never Take our Freedommmmmmmm` Brave heart movie one of our Scottish hero`s brought a smile to my face.

As the IV/IG is a blood product I had to sign a consent form as the doc told me that there was a risk of the blood being contaminated. One of the risks would be contracting `AIDS`, however the risk was very slight. And the good news just keeps on coming! It sure is an up and down journey this.

Next drugs to be prescribed were Prednisolone (Steroid) and Azathioprine (Immunosuppressant). These 2 drugs I had taken before for the first few years of my lupus. I had been told then that I would be on them for life. However 6 years later I came off them so I wasn't worried too much. I knew the side effects were not too bad and that I could handle them without too much trouble.

On top of these I was prescribed Pyridostigmine or Mestinon. This is a drug primarily for Myasthenia Gravis. In MG the muscles quickly tire and weaken, this is caused by excessive activity in the body of a protein called cholinesterase. Mestinon belongs to a group of medicines known as `Cholinesterase inhibitors`. Mestinon boosts the signal between nerve and muscle so that acetylcholine (the chemical signal released from the nerve) has longer to activate the muscle. Acetylcholine is broken down by cholinesterase. If you inhibit the cholinesterase, the acetylcholine lasts longer.

No one seems sure whether Mestinon is of much use to LEMS patients but hey we are desperate here. `Don`t knock it until you`ve tried it` seems to be the attitude.

Next to add to my growing list is a drug that is specifically just for LEMS It is called 3, 4- Dap (Diaminopyridine) or Amifampridine.

With LEMS the message from the nerve to the muscle doesn`t connect, therefore the muscle cannot work. To get technical about it a chemical called Acetyl-choline, which communicates nerve impulses to muscles is not released normally and the muscle doesn`t receive some or all of the nerves signals. The way 3, 4- Dap works is by releasing more of the Acetylcholine helping the muscles to receive the nerve signals. The doctor explained that it is a bit like how the choke in your car works. What worries me is `Will it flood my engine? `

There is a lot of ballyhoo surrounding 3, 4- Dap. Apparently this drug is only made by one company. It used to cost around £3,000 a year per patient. However the company decided to license it and are now able to charge whatever they like. The price has now gone up to an exorbitant £60,000 a year. Ouch! Of course some P.C.T `s will not be keen to approve it. So it is your post code lottery again. Without this drug you are not going to get your life back.

Southampton hospital gets around this problem by giving their patients the unlicensed version .All legal so I'm informed. However I have this comical image of the roof tops or basements of this hospital resembling a druggie's attic bursting at the seams with illegal cannabis looking drug plantations. Expecting a raid anytime now from the Drug Squad.

The only problem here is that once I leave this hospital I can no longer be given their version of the drug. Therefore Dr B has written to my P.C.T in Portsmouth to ask for approval. God I hope they think I'm worth it.

We're not finished yet? All these drugs can cause havoc with your poor stomach so Dr B prescribed another drug to protect the stomach lining `Lanzoprazole`. Next 2 drugs to protect your bones (side effect of high steroid use is bone thinning) Alendronate and Calcichew and don't forget to add on the nightly stomach injection to stop the Deep Vein Thrombosis.

So there I was a walking medicine cabinet. The nurses would be around several times a day with the `Ice Cream Trolley` I Wish! That's what it looked like until they unlocked the lid and dished out my quota. All of which had to be crushed, mixed with water and syringed up my nose. At least I wouldn't taste them I guess.

The dietician came to say they would start me on 1,000 kc a day then gradually work up to 1,500kc. As I had lost so much weight so quickly they were worried about re- feeding syndrome. They explained what that was.

During WW2 when the troops liberated the prisoner of war camps they saw how emaciated and starving those poor souls were and gave them lots of food thinking it would help them recover. What happened next however made the doctors realise that because their stomachs had shrunk so much the food made them very ill. The doctors then had to feed them up gradually to allow the stomachs to expand back to normal. As I had not been overweight to begin with I had become extremely thin, in fact catching a glimpse of myself in the bathroom mirror had given me grave cause for concern. Never in my life had I seen my bones protruding like they were. I looked like one of those skeletal super models. Now that is scary.

So the calories would be monitored and increased slowly. The only food I was having was a liquid feed which of course had to go up my snout. It looked like a frappe, thankfully I couldn't taste it as I bet it didn't taste like a frappe. I had visions of never being able to eat normally again.

S.a.l.t came again to check on me and she asked me if I was aware of my white coated tongue, was it giving me any pain or discomfort? I said I had noticed it but it wasn't bothering me in any way I just thought it was the drugs and not being able to drink. She suggested `Nystatin` a mouth wash to prevent me getting mouth thrush. Heck I thought my med list was complete? Here we go yet another drug.

I tried the mouth wash and it tasted foul so that went in the bin and I decided to try something else. I thought I would try tongue brushing. I had heard that you could either use your toothbrush or a tongue scraper I used the latter. Although it would be hard not to gag when you reach in to the back of your tongue as I had no gag reflex at the moment I was able to scrape right to the back. It worked a treat, my old pink tongue returned. They're so quick to prescribe drugs why don't they let you try the natural remedy first? It makes my blood boil.

Later that day Maxine (my vegan friend) who is a fully qualified Veterinary Surgeon and also a Hippocrates Health Trainer who specializes in Nutrition came to see me and bring me some of her Wheatgrass Juice. She grows this organically and juices it herself. I unscrewed the flask top; it smelt gorgeous, like a freshly mowed lawn and reminded me of how much I am missing the outside world. I thought will they allow me to put this up my NG though`?

I remembered that Max's Wheatgrass juice had come to my rescue before in December 2008.

Four years ago I'd been unlucky enough to contract Shingles for the 2nd time in my life. This time though instead of being on my back it was in my left eye following the trigeminal nerve up the side of my nose up to the left eye and then up and over the left side of my head. I had never had to endure so much pain in my life. The medication didn't seem to help much. It felt like I was being stabbed in the eye with a red hot needle and my whole left side of my face and head burned, I was having to put ice packs over my face and head which made me feel that I just wanted to die so the pain would go. What made it all worse that it was Christmastime and of course getting to see a G.P during the holidays was almost impossible?

I was given steroid cream to put into my eye by the doctor at the eye hospital and told that I might lose the sight in that eye, and that the eye would be permanently drooped. I was horrified. There must be something I could do?

I phoned Max. A few days later she rang me and said she wanted to try something. So there I was cycling down in the snow to Max's veterinary practice to pick up some ice cubes of wheatgrass that she had prepared for me. I cycled home with my cool bag over my shoulder and transferred my 'prescription' into my freezer. Wheatgrass is a power house of anti-oxidants .I was to defrost 1 cube daily and use it all as eyewash. Hey what could I lose? I was willing to try anything. So for 3 weeks I washed my eye out with the gorgeous smelling liquid, 1 cube gave me enough for 3 washes.

At my follow up visit to the eye department the doctor was amazed that I still had my sight and that the droop had gone completely. I had a little bit of scarring at the back of my eye but through some miracle I had maintained my vision.

I didn't tell them that it was no miracle. If I'd told them what I'd been doing I think they would have thrown a wobbly. Doctors are never very open to alternative medicines as I've found out over the last 20 years. However I came out of that hospital grinning like a Cheshire cat! I thought why not a cat ha-ha. After all it was a Veterinary who had saved my sight.

On reflection did you know that a veterinary spends a year studying nutrition to look after animals and a GP is lucky if they study for a couple of hours to look after us humans? Need I say more?

Well Max asks the nurse if she could put the juice up my NG after explaining what it was. The nurse agreed. I was amazed because I had asked the dietician if I could put my vitamin powders mixed with water up a few days ago and she was adamant that only water, drugs and feed were allowed. Well I had told the nurses that I'd got the ok on this and had been having my powders syringed up my nose since last week. Okay so my nose had grown another inch heehee.

When the docs came around I asked them all if I could get some information on this LEMS I told them that I need to know what I'm fighting here, know who my enemy is so I can fight back .Dr Ash said he would come and have a chat with me after he finished work as a friend not a doctor. Hmm that sounds ominous, I don't think they want me to have any information, what are they hiding from me?

Later Dr Ash came as promised. We had a chat for the best part of an hour. He told me that he would find me some information but that he didn't want me to look it up on the internet as it made for very scary reading. Mmmmm? As I`d never had a computer there was no chance of that anyway.

It had been a very interesting day so far and I couldn't wait for Bob to get home from work so as I could phone with the good news, this wasn't one of his visiting days and we didn`t have a mobile phone. (Got one now)

It was difficult for me to walk the few steps to the nurses' station to use the phone. I slumped down into a chair. Having no muscles working you could not believe how difficult it was to pick up the phone hold it to my ear and talk. My speech sounded as if I was drunk and I didn't sound like me at all. It was hard to get the words out. I had to keep the message short and sweet. It was so good to hear Bobs voice on the other end and I managed to get `Good news babe, they know what is wrong with me. ` I burst into tears. I told Bob I was exhausted and this would have to be a short call. He wrote down the name of this `intruder` Lambert Eaton Myasthenic Syndrome which I had to spell out with great difficulty having a mouth and tongue that was hardly moving. He sounded elated told me to go and get some rest and that he loved me so much and looked forward to seeing me tomorrow. I was physically and emotionally exhausted but managed to get back to bed. 40 minutes later I had a phone call.

It was Jules my neighbour and running buddy. Great news Deb! She hollers down the phone. I smiled `Sounds like you're having a party there` to which she laughs` we are, your Bob and Pete and me, we`ve opened a bottle of bubbly. We're all going to get sloshed to celebrate.

Bob had popped in to tell them the good news and they took one look at his face and pulled him in for a Hugs and Hooch. It was so good to hear him in the background laughing and enjoying the frivolities. Julie told me Pete was going to look on the internet and see what he could find. Weeks later Pete told me of his dismay on what he found. `I can't show this to Bob` he exclaimed.

I decided there and then to get out my boxing gloves and get back in the ring, after all I`ve done it before. I had battled with the `wolf` Latin for lupus. I had learnt to make a friend of him and had been running with the pack rather than from the pack for 14 years.

`Get your thoughts right and the physical must follow`

Now I see the LEMS as a sly fox sneaking up on me. Well I see you coming you bushy tailed critter and I'm ready. You can't frighten me.

I remember 21 years ago almost funnily enough to the day when I was diagnosed with Lupus (Systemic Lupus Erythematosus) it was autumn 1991.

I had awoken on the Saturday morning unable to uncurl from the foetal position I slept in. I ached all over, had pains in my chest and felt stiff as a board. `What the hell's going on here I thought have I had a stroke?

I managed to drag myself to the phone and rang the GP (not my own) my GP shared Saturday morning with a nearby practice which happened luckily enough to be at the bottom of my street.

I spent 2 hours with the doc being prodded and poked, questioned and then wired up to a heart machine. Eventually I was given a sealed letter put in an ambulance and wheeled into Accident and Emergency.

The receptionist read the letter and all hell let loose. 'Quick get this patient into cubicle now!' She hollered. I had been jumped in front of a full waiting room and was instantly surrounded by 3 doctors. What was in that letter I never did find out but it had them all worried. Anyway 2 more hours of tests and questions went by.

Then a doctor came in looking very serious. 'There's Good News and there's Bad News.' He said. First the Good news is we know what's wrong with you. The bad news is you have ****-/-- bla bla bla. I'd never heard of it I asked him to repeat it. Systemic Lupus Erythematososis. My God that sounded scary and the look on his face told me it was very serious. 'How Long Have I Got?' I said. Those were my actual words.

'Oh it's not that bad. Although, 20 years ago you wouldn't have made 50, but now with the medications we have you could live longer than that.' Jeesussss I'm only 32 but 50 is not that far away and it's certainly too young to die. He then adds 'You will have to Modify Your Lifestyle somewhat though' Modify my lifestyle what does he mean by that?

Somehow I don't think that doctor meant Take up Running but hey that's exactly what I did, although not right away.

On release from A&E an appointment was made for me with Rheumatology. The following week (they didn't hang about) I found myself being told by the Rheumatology Consultant that I was Auto –Immune. My body was attacking itself. SLE was an auto immune disease and it was incurable. Once again I was told I would have to' modify my lifestyle' I would feel very tired a lot of the time and I would need lots of rest.

I was also told that I would have to take drugs for the rest of my life. For someone who had never even taken an aspirin in her life this news really did knock me for six. I was telling the Consultant all the strange things I had been experiencing over the past months. E.g.: Headaches, missed periods, blurred vision, swollen joints, mouth and finger ulcers to name a few. I had also had a very strange experience.

A few weeks ago I had been doing a bit of temp waitressing work in a local hotel. I had cleared a dirty table and gone into the wash up in the kitchen. What happened next was what I can only describe as an' out of body experience.'

I found myself putting the cutlery down the food waste disposal and the food into the cutlery trough. The kitchen porter was throwing a wobbly and I can't repeat the swear words he was shouting at me. The weirdest thing is I could see myself doing these things but couldn't seem to stop myself. It was as if I had stepped out of my body and I was watching myself from the side-lines. The doctor listened patiently then told me that this was due quite worryingly to inflammation on the brain. How scary is that?

I was prescribed an array of medications. Steroids, immunosuppressant's, anti-inflammatory, anti-malarial, anti-psychotics' and a few others to make up a cocktail of drugs and told I would also have to have regular blood tests and eye tests to make sure the drugs were not doing any damage. The side effects all sounded pretty grim, but hey what choice did I have?

Months later chatting with another Lupus patient she told me of a similar incident which happened to her which was very funny. She had come home from shopping and was putting the new socks she had bought for her husband in the freezer and the fish was going into the sock drawer. Heehee we were both in stiches as we recalled our experiences. Well, you've got to have a sense of humour to cope with illness.

My life from that day on was on a downward spiral. All I could do was struggle through my work day and come home to get into bed. I had absolutely no energy at all. Bob would wake me to feed me and I would go straight back to bed again. I would watch Bob bouncing around full of life, he would go for a run come back full of health and vitality. I felt all the negative emotions, Anger, Frustration, Fury, Resentment, Sorrow, and Bitterness. `This is not my life`

It was a living nightmare for the next few years of trying to find the right concoction of drugs for me which would cause the least hassle from the awful side effects. I thought to myself `There has got to be another way? `

So I decided I would do my own research. I would read up all I could get my hands on about this disease. At the time internet was all quite new and not everyone had access to it. However I had a brother working in a hospital in Saudi Arabia who managed to get me loads of information. I soaked it all up. Next I scoured the charity shops, jumble sales and libraries to pick up any books on Alternative therapies and Nutrition and read them all taking notes as I went. Lastly I decided that I had to do some exercise.

 I had always wanted to train to be an exercise instructor so why don't I just do it. Even if I can't teach I will have the knowledge to help work myself out a programme. So in 1995 I enrolled for a year's part time course with the Keep Fit Association and went ahead.

It was hard work. Every 2nd Saturday I would take a train to Salisbury for a full day of exercise and theory. I also had to attend night school to do a Teacher Training Certificate course, the 7306. Well a year went by and I passed all my exams and I was now a fully qualified exercise teacher. I was thrilled as I'd never been much good at school so this qualification meant a lot to me. I knew that being on long term steroids would destroy my bone density and there would be a grave possibility that I would end up with osteoporosis. I also knew now with my training and research that I could do a lot to combat this loss with good nutrition and weight bearing exercise.

At the time I was working in a hotel which was fortunate enough to have a gym and a pool with a spa which the staff where allowed to use as a perk. So three days a week I would literally drag myself in there after work. I got so fit that I was able to come off all my medication. The Consultant wasn't happy to take me off but I insisted that I felt so good I wanted to try for a while without the drugs and see how I got on. So he reluctantly agreed. He was seeing me in a few months anyway so we could review it then.

The Gym was a small friendly club and it didn't have any T.V. No one had mp3 players like they do today. People spoke to one another. It was a very sociable environment to work out in and it suited me fine.

It so happened that the days I was in the gym coincided with the days Arthur a Portsmouth Jogger was in there training. He would usually be on the treadmill next to me he would be running and I would be walking. Over the next 3 months Arthur would encourage me to first walk/run then run chatting the whole time about all sorts of things. Eventually I found myself running non-stop for 3 miles which was about half an hour. I was amazed. Then one day I came into the gym all the treadmills were in use so Arthur suggested I run outside along the seafront. I took off. It was a beautiful, cool fresh sunny day. I couldn't believe how much easier it was to run outside. There was so much to focus on. There were the sounds of the waves crashing up onto the pebble beach, the seagulls crying and a flock of starlings whistling as they swirled overhead, the trees and shrubs as I ran past the rock gardens. The scenery changing as I ran, this was much better than looking at myself in a mirror in the gym.

When I got back Arthur asked me where I got to, when I told him, he gasped `you've just ran 5 miles! ` We were both amazed. Wow! That was it. No more treadmill for me. I went from strength to strength. The next few months I worked hard, I was running 3 times a week and also doing the weight machines in the gym. The best thing of all was that I felt I was putting up a good fight with my Lupus.

I could now run for 8 miles non-stop so I decided to enter the Great South Run in October 1998. That was my first official running race. Bob had already entered a while ago never dreaming that I would be there with him. You see I hadn't told him. I was secretly running and I wanted to surprise him. It worked; he was gobsmacked when I told him about a fortnight before that I was in.

The big day arrived I must admit although excited I was very nervous as I'd only done 8 miles, I just accepted the fact that I would probably have to walk the last 2 miles. I was lucky to hitch up with another girl who was also doing her first race and we ran together chatting and laughing the whole way around. We were so engrossed that before we knew it we were coming up to the finish line 10 miles we'd Done it Yahooooo!!!!! We crossed the line holding hands and both burst into tears and fell into each other's arms. What a day. Sadly I've never seen her since but I do hope she is still running. I didn't take that medal off for weeks.

The following day was my check up with Dr T, my Rheumatology consultant. I am certain he was expecting me to crawl in and beg to be put back on the meds. However I walked or should I say bounced into the consulting room grinning from ear to ear.

`How have you been? 'he asks `well, ` I said as I pulled out my medal ` I did this yesterday` he took the medal and looked at it `The Great South Run, but that's ten miles!' he gasped `It sure is and I did it in 2 hours non-stop running` I beamed.

I must admit I did feel smug. His mouth gaped open and he almost fell off his chair. `I was going to suggest a blood test

but I don't think we need bother it looks like you're doing ok without the drugs, Well Done.`

I am lucky that I have the sort of personality that makes me a fighter. If someone tells me I can't do something it`s like a Red rag to a Bull to me `Yeah We`ll see about that` is my usual response. Bob always jokes `No one tells my wife what to do` ha-ha.

So that was the start of my 14 years without medication until I got hit with the LEMS.

Saturday 19th November.

Didn`t sleep much. I had too much going through my head. Will I work again? Will I be in a wheelchair? Will I have to move house or get a stair lift put in? Will I be on Disability the rest of my life? Will I ever lead a normal life again? Will I have to give away all of my running kit? Will they find Cancer?

I was started on the IV/IG today which went in through a cannula in my arm. In go the `Hired Thugs` as Alan Rickman puts in Robin Hood Prince of Thieves. Go to it Lads!

The cannula was very painful when it was being put in. The nurse tried three times and failed miserably so she called the doctor to do it. It was in and we`re off. If I had a pound for every needle that's been stuck into me I'll be rich by the time I get out of here. I gloomily thought if I get out of here?

The nurse gave me a fizzy pain killer which played havoc with my Hiatus hernia. Now I had a stomach ache as well as a head ache. What have I done to deserve all this?

`This is not my life`

Being on a drip is a real pain in the ass. Everywhere you go the tripod stand, which is on wheels, has to go too. I felt like Fred Astaire with his hat stand although I certainly didn't feel like dancing. I was desperately trying to push the stand without tripping myself up and it required great effort. So for the next five days on the IV/IG where I went Fred went too, I felt like Ginger Rogers. I got so used to taking the thing everywhere I went that one night I had been unplugged for the night but still took the damn thing with me to the loo. The girls on the ward had a good laugh. What an idiot!

Sunday 20th November.

Bob is coming today. I was hoping he could take me out for some fresh air but with being tied up to Fred that wasn`t very practical. I had also been having trouble with the feed that the nurses had been syringing up my NG. I don't know what they put in that stuff but my stomach was not very keen to accept it .It would take a couple of days to settle down. In the meantime I had to have a commode at my bedside. How humiliating. As soon as the nurse put the first feed of the day in I was up and running and I don`t mean a 10km or a half marathon if you get my drift? Will it be a nappy next?

My weight had slipped down even more and I now weighed 8stone 3lb and I looked gaunt and very unwell.

My once well-toned runner's legs were very thin and my well-toned butt had gone south looking very saggy and baggy. My heart sank.

All my feed, water and drugs were being fed in by the nurses. One of the drugs gave me a tingling feeling around my mouth, like I had just used very strong toothpaste. It wasn't unpleasant just weird.

I hadn't slept much at all in the last eleven days and I longed for deep restful sleep. I had bags under my eyes that I could've taken on holiday. They`d have charged me `excess baggage`. The ward was quiet at the weekends. Many of the patients went home on Friday night and returned early Monday morning. I was astonished. It`s ridiculous when you think about it. Two days every week nothing happens in here. No scans, no physiotherapy, no blood test, and no consultants. There was just one doctor on at the weekend and it was often a junior and he wouldn't do the rounds. You only saw him if there was a problem. No wonder we are all in here for so long? It`s Crazy!

I am listening to my Christmas choral music. I have always loved the run up to Christmas and I`m feeling sorry for myself being stuck in here. I wonder if I'll get home for Christmas.

It was so good to see Bob. Now that we knew what was wrong with me we felt we were getting on the right track back to health. Although we were both very much aware of the impending scans I had to come.

Monday 21st November

 Bob brought me loads of get well cards from friends and the string they were on that surrounded my bed was growing. When it was time for him to go my heart felt heavy. It would be another couple of days before I saw him again.

I was having a bad night again. I woke up several times with my mouth full of foamy saliva, choking and panicky. I had to press the emergency button for the nurses to come and help me as I couldn't lift my arm up high enough to reach the oxygen mask that was above my head. They also turned on the sucker to clear the saliva. There was one good thing though. My stomach had become used to the feed and after two days the commode could go.

At home I always sleep in the nude, so I had been wearing `prison issue` bright orange hospital pyjamas. They were `one size fits all` and I had a job keeping the bottoms on. I had rolled up the trouser legs several times so that I wouldn't trip over them. These things were enormous. I looked like a clown. If you've ever seen the film south pacific `one hundred and one balls of fun` you'll get the picture.

More blood tests, another cannula to go in as this one was beginning to hurt. First attempt my vein bulged up, the nurse tried the other arm, vein collapsed. She then went back to other arm. It's in at last. Thank god! Next the nurse syringes in my feed up my NG Tube. The problem with this is that a lot of feed is going into me at one time and on an empty stomach too. I am used to eating `little and often` so consequently after each feed I felt nauseous. This would freak me out as I had visions of the crash team and the oxygen mask caper all over again.

The other problem with the nurse being responsible for everything that went up my NG was that just wanting a simple drink of water turned into a major incident. Firstly you had to find a nurse. She would say be with you in a minute, you wait, ask again, and feel guilty for seeking their attention when you could see they were busy. One day it was 13 hours without food or water which had me climbing the walls with frustration and I ended up with a massive migraine for the rest of the day and night. There has got to be a better way.

All 5 Doctors came around again to say still waiting for a slot for scans. They asked me if I would be willing to be a guinea pig for the students this week. Why not? I thought one of these smart young people might be the one who finds a cure. Bring them on I said.

In the afternoon the porter came to take me to x ray. He shouts `Taxi for Deborah Pentland ` as he swings the wheelchair up to my bedside `The scenic route please driver` I joked.

Later as the nurse was trying to get as much of the two feed bags into me for my daily calorie quota I had to say` no more I can't handle it. It's making me feel so sick` It was only 1,000 kc and I couldn't cope with it. How am I going to put my weight back on? Everyone around me is eating and drinking and I get sludge squirted up my snout. `This is not my life`

In fact the amount of food people have in here is ridiculous. I would imagine that most patients go home having put on weight just sitting in bed all day and packing away breakfast, lunch and dinner, morning coffee and biscuits, afternoon tea and cake, and then as if that's not enough there is hot chocolate and cookies for supper. Not to mention `Burger King` down in the lobby. It's far too much.

Nurses having trouble getting reading on my `ob.'s ` again. I also have Raynaud's disease. This means that my extremities have a problem with getting a blood supply as the vessels go into spasm. They turn white, blue and then red. It might be very patriotic but a real nuisance and very painful when the blood finally does push its way through. Consequently my hands and feet and are often cold and as the oxygen levels are read by a peg that goes on your finger, or your toes I have no reading. It would become a standing joke with the nurses `You`re dead`

Tuesday 22nd November

We had a bit of excitement today. I felt sorry for the poor student nurse who had been asked to take my `obs` this morning. She became very anxious when my pulse read 240. Eh! I don't think so? Even when I'm in full flight running mode the highest it would be was 138. The Sister on hearing her exclamation quickly came over to assure her it was not at it appeared. ` What is it with you and machines `the Sister said? `

The IV/IG is on its fourth day. Can't say I feel any benefit but the doc did say that it can take 2 to 3 weeks to take effect. I can feel a tingling sensation in my arms though. I thought the `army` are on the move.

I had a word with the dietician about my feeding problems. She suggested putting the feed on a drip. This way it would be a more gradual feeding and it would be put on in the morning and would slowly feed me for the next 12 hours. As I got used to it I could speed it up and have it on for a shorter time. I could also pause and unplug it if I had visitors and I would be able to go outside for fresh air. That idea sounded great.

I had the students around again. They were on the wards for two weeks so every day I would see a fresh batch of eager budding doctors all examining and asking me questions. LEMS being so rare, they were milking it. I was pushed, pulled, prodded, and poked for two hours on one occasion. It was too much I was exhausted. However at the end of the session the consultant asks the students to have a go at a diagnosis. One bright young lass says firmly `lambert Eaton` the doc looks at her very curiously ` are you sure, do you know how rare that is? She stuck by her decision and was rewarded with a hearty well done. Maybe she will be the one to find a cure?

The Physiotherapists are coming to see others on the ward. When can I get moving again, I thought? For someone so used to exercise not being able to move was really awful and with the doctors telling me that exercise can make LEMS worse is really playing on my psyche.

<u>Wednesday 23rd November.</u>

More students today but doc kept it to ½ hour. I think he felt guilty after yesterday's session. One of the doctors asked if he could come back later to examine me again. He had recently qualified and was now going to specialize in `Neuro-Science` and he had never met anyone with LEMS before. He kept saying how special I was. Yeah right. I don't want to be special I just want to be normal.

He came back later to do some reflex testing on me. He would knock my knee with the small hammer- nothing. He then asked me to hold my leg up off the bed this would work the muscle. It was very hard to do. Then he tested the reflex again. Apparently by holding the leg up I was flooding the muscle with calcium so it would become stronger. I didn't understand the technicality of it all but I would like to try. I asked Dr D if he could get me some information on LEMS. He looked very doubtful but said he would try. Not for the first time I thought what are they hiding from me?

It is my last day of the IV/IG .A five day course of this stuff costs around £ 3,000 Thank God for the N.H.S. Imagine having to cough up the cash for this lot I am having in here?

Bob arrived with Gary. Bob had another load of cards for me with very moving words in some of them from my friends and people from my exercise classes. One of my lovely ladies had even enclosed a cheque for £100 to go towards my next charity event. I usually raise funds for Lupus or Raynaud's but I think this will go towards Myasthenia.

The specialist nurse came around to have a chat. Her salary is paid for by the Myasthenia Gravis Association so my next fundraising monies will be well spent.

She is one of only 7 specialist nurses in the UK. She had never met anyone with LEMS before so she didn't know too much about it, but told me what she knew.

It didn't sound too good at all. Of course she said that no two patients were the same but all this talk of taking it easy, exercise can make it worse, and offers of help to fill in the benefit forms didn't fill me with much hope. It all sounded much scarier than my Lupus, when I was told I would have to `modify my life style` Well. That phrase had got me into running, so I wasn't going to give up my life that easily. I told her that I would get back to running; I know she didn't believe it. However I did and that was all that mattered. Bob would have said if he had heard her. `Ah but you don`t know my wife. No one tells her what she can and can`t do` I told the nurse that I will run again and I will send her a photo so that the next poor soul she meets who has just been diagnosed with LEMS will have a positive example of the` life after diagnosis. ` `If we think we can or think we can`t we`re right` I don`t think she believed me and she just smiled.

Fourteen years ago after six years on drugs for my Lupus I had proved them all wrong. I would prove that I would not have to take medication for the rest of my life by coming off all of my drugs. I had been told that no one lives with lupus without drugs. Well I had for 14 years and on top of that I had run over 400 hundred races, 12 of them marathons, lots of half marathons and many 10 mile and 10km`s. Telling me I can`t do something is I'm afraid like a `Red rag to a Bull`.

I remember my very first marathon. It was 2001, 2 ½ years after my very first run the Great South. I saw an advert in the gym asking for runners to raise funds for `Hearing dogs for the deaf`. Bob had always wanted to run the London Marathon and he had a place already. So I phoned them up. I had a chat with a nice lady who told me all about what these dogs do and how they made such a difference to deaf people. Yep, Count me in I thought. I just had to raise funds for this wonderful cause. I would run, walk or crawl my way around those 26.2 miles .I could not imagine what it would be like to not hear the thing`s I cherished. Imagine not being able to hear birds singing, waves splashing or crashing onto the rocks on the beach, a flock of geese flying overhead or the sound of a crackling fire. That was all the incentive I needed.

The training was hard work. I had seen a plan in runner's world magazine and I decided to follow that as closely as I could. That would hopefully get me around in less than 5 hours. That was my goal.

I must admit there were times when I didn't feel up to either the training run or the gym but with encouragement from all my family and friends I was spurred on. Running with Lupus is like running in a suit of chain mail our energy levels can drop extremely low and everything becomes such an effort. A marathon was 26.2 miles, the furthest I'd run in training was the recommended 20 miles. So it's `Ready or not here I come`

Well eventually the Big Day arrived. Bob had somehow managed to get injured a few weeks previously so I was on my own. It was very emotional .I waved Bob goodbye and boarded the runners bus from our hotel to take us to the start line. Bob would see me at the finishing straight along the Mall. I just didn't know how I was going to cope with it all. But I need not have worried.

The day was just amazing. I could sprawl on for ages but instead I will show you the poem I wrote afterwards that says it all.

My First London Marathon

The training done, it wasn`t always fun,
Early morning runs without the sun.
Rain, sleet, cold winds and snowing
For six long months the biting winds blowing.

Then around it came. The big day had arrived.
The flu, the colds, and the viruses I'd survived.
I`m at the start line, huddled in the crowd,
Oh if I can do this won`t I feel proud.

We`re off! The Wombles, the clown, the Viking ship,
The rhino, the trees, the banana- don`t slip.
The crowds are so loud. The hoots and the cheers.
A couple of fairies stop off for some beers.

A group of policeman run after a crook.
A man in a bear suit, then Captain Hook.
The miles pass by. I spot a friend.
Tower Bridge is around this bend.

Brilliant! Half Way! We`re on our way back.
To a hug, a kiss, a cuppa a snack.
15, 16, 17 miles done,
18, 19, and 20 I've run.

Oh No! It`s the wall! I`ve heard about that,
But I'd followed Runners World advice so forget about that.
21, 22, 23 the dreaded cobbles.
Look out! Smile at the camera and try not to wobble.

Smile! OK grin as you pass on your way.
Onto the finish and you hope and you pray
Along the embankment a couple get wed
Oh God, I could do with my bed!

Big Ben strikes, no more breathe to talk,
Around the bend into Bird cage walk
The crowd going wild, the noise doesn`t diminish,
Down the mall and on to the finish.

Arms in the air, tears rolling down,
Yes I can do it, I can beat that clown
Under the arch, over the line.
I`ve done it! 26 miles and I feel fine.

After running my first marathon I felt Invincible, Indestructible. I had slayed my Dragon. I had also raised £1,800 for Hearing Dogs for the Deaf. Oh! And I did it in 4hour 33 minutes. I walked around for about two weeks grinning from ear to ear and I hardly took the medal off. I was so proud of myself.

`He who conquers others is strong
But he who conquers himself if Mighty`

Thursday24rth November

Slept until around 3am when I awoke extremely thirsty, my mouth felt like sandpaper. The nurse syringed in a few cups of water. God, I never thought that I could appreciate a simple drink of good old H $_2$O. There is a lot of ballyhoo when using an NG tube. Before anything goes up the tube you have to`aspirate` This involves a complicated caper of first syringing up out of the stomach a drop of liquid, which you then put on a strip of litmus paper which has to read less than 5 acidity /alkaline level. If not then you can't put anything in. You then have to swab the mouth with a sponge on a stick dipped in apple or orange juice, wait 15 minutes or so and try again. By which time I'm absolutely gasping for a drink. I feel as if I`ve been stranded in the desert for days. My reading was nearly always over 5. Weeks later about 3 days before I was due to go home I found out that my reading was always going to be high because of one of the damn drugs I was on. So I had endured that entire caper for weeks unnecessarily. Why don't the nurses read your notes?

I had a major break -through today. I can slide my arm up over my head while lying in bed. It`s hard work but I can do it.

I am going for a C.T. Scan today. I had been awoken at 6am as I had to have 2 litres of orange squash up through my tube; apparently the dye helps to show things more clearly in the scan. As the nurse was syringing it in I felt as if I was going to burst! My stomach felt like a barrage balloon.

The porter came to take me down `scenic route` I am left sitting in the corridor alongside an old lady who has been wheeled down still in her bed. I saw a nurse walking towards me with a tray holding another 2 litre jug of juice. Good God If I have any more I'll explode I thought as I shrank back into my wheelchair. Thankfully another nurse called out `Not that one, the other patient` Phew, that was close I had visions of bits of me splattered all over the walls. Messy!

The door opened and I saw a sterile looking room with what I can only describe as a massive ring donut. That is the scanner. I was wheeled over to the table, asked to lie down on my back and make myself comfortable. A Radiographer chap explains what will happen. `You will feel the warm saline we inject into your cannula gradually seeping through your body, when it reaches your hips you will feel as if you have wet yourself. Don`t worry you won`t have, stay perfectly still and listen to the automated voice and follow the instructions. The whole procedure will take about 20 minutes. I closed my eyes. I must admit to being a little frightened.

It was very noisy, like a jumbo jet taking off. The table that I lay on was sliding into the donut. The voice says `Breathe normally` The bed felt as if it was swaying and when the warm saline hit my hips it was just like I had wet myself. It took me back to my wind surfing lessons when the instructor had told us all to pee in the wet suit to keep us warm. There I was, my eyes closed imagining myself down at the beach windsurfing, enjoying the day, not a care in the world. It was great. It was almost a shame when it came to an end.

All done, two staff had to help me up as I couldn't do it myself. I was told to drink lots of water to flush out the dye. I wasn`t allowed any caffeine. Huh, chance would be a fine thing.

Had a shower when I got back to the ward and I actually managed to do a bit myself. I could at least wash the front of my body, the nurse had to do my hair and back and dress me. But hey it is an improvement all be it a small one. I caught a glimpse of myself in the mirror. Ugh I look like a skeleton. By now I was down to 8 stone. I hadn't been that weight since my school days!

The nurse came to do my `obs`. My lung capacity had dropped down to 1.36 it should read 3.5 for my size and fitness.

Thinking about my next scan I am worried as I now know they are looking for Cancer. I`m scared.

S.a.l.t tried me on stewed apple it took me 25 minutes to get about an egg cup full down. She told me I was to have cold custard or yogurt. They all had to be cold as the cold stimulated the muscles in the throat and assisted the swallow. So breakfast, lunch and dinner was custard, yogurt and stewed apple.

After a couple of days I realised that the dairy products were clogging up my sinuses and making it even harder to breathe so I was reduced to stewed apple. How exciting.

Friday 25th November.

One month until Christmas. This is normally my favourite time of year. The whole run up, the music, the decorations, the trees, and the concerts, the whole atmosphere and I was missing it all. Being in here is as if Christmas is not happening.

Yippee I showered on my own today, sitting on the chair in the wet room I even managed to do my back by throwing the towel over my shoulder but it was exhausting. I found it all more tiring than running a marathon. I had to have a lie down afterwards to recover.

Saturday 26th November

The doctor came to tell me that the C.T. Scan was clear apart from a very small raisin size blob under my right arm. As the nurse pulled the curtain around my bed the doc told me he wanted to do a manual breast examination. There I was naked from the waist up with my right arm wedged behind my head. The doctor's face was a few inches from mine. He has a good feel around. I had to bite my tongue from saying `Does this mean we`re engaged`. He found the raisin, took my finger to show me. It was tiny. I was to have another scan so it could be thoroughly checked out. This time it would be a P.E.T Scan. This would check my body at cellular level.

Later I had one bit of good news. My lung function test was 2.12 a PB `Personal Best`.

Dr D who had been with me in the muscle testing examination room where they finally got the diagnosis asked if I would mind being the subject of a talk that he was to give next month to a group of Consultants. Again he was telling me how special I was. Hmmmmm. He wanted to video a muscle testing examination with me that he could use it for his talk. Fame at last.

Bob came after work today. He is running in the Hayling ten mile race tomorrow. This is a run that we were supposed to be running together. I cried myself to sleep again when he left.

Sunday 27th November.

Anita my Physiotherapy friend came to spend the day with me. Anita wheeled me down to the café so we could go outside and sit by the tree which was almost bare now. She made me walk through the café which is only about 10 metres or so but I found it very difficult. I felt as if my legs would give out from beneath me. If they did I couldn't stop myself from falling as my arms were still useless. The thought of breaking a bone really worried me. Eventually we made it and we sat chatting for ages. It was so good to be out in the fresh air.

We reminisced about last year when we had all done the Hayling 10 Mile run together and how we had sat in my camper van afterwards having tea and watching the snow falling. Anita had a calf injury and was feeling sad because she would miss the run. I told her that at least she wasn't stuck in here. That cheered her up.

As we were walking back into the café it was beginning to fill up with people all tucking into real food. Guess what I had to look forward to? Yep, Apple puree and a bag of sludge up my nose. I can`t wait!

Monday 29th November

I awoke with a headache. If only I could get a good night's sleep. I did manage to shower on my own today. I reckon I must be improving although the progress is so slow and minimal. Again it did take a lot out of me. I would never have thought that a mere shower would knacker me so.

I actually managed to sip a small glass of water today and ooh it tasted so good. Jan, a lovely lady on the ward was in for her regular IV/IG 5 day treatment. She was having it to treat her low level cancer. The first day she arrived as soon as she was unpacked she announces she was off outside for fag. I couldn't believe my ears. `You're joking ` I said. Later that day her daughter and beautiful little granddaughter came to see her. Her granddaughter was 5 years old and cried her eyes out as she was about to leave she sobbed `I don't want nana to die` Well, she had me in tears too. After they left I said to Jan .` You've got to give up the fags girl if you want to see that lovely granddaughter of yours grow up get married 'She told me she had been wanting to stop.' Start now' I said.

I`m glad to say that Jan didn`t have another cigarette from that day on. A few days later when the doctors were seeing her just before her release they too told her that she had to give up the fags. `Oh I've already given up haven't had one for last 4 days, Deb talked me out of it. ` Ha ha the doctor looks over to me and says` I think we should keep you in here and move you around the wards` I was always telling people to give up. If I ran past a smoker I would always shout out with a smile `Do yourself a favour, stub em out my friend` I couldn't help myself, my own father had died of lung cancer from heavy smoking in his 50`s I knew the consequences. It`s a mugs game. Of course I don't know if she kept it up but I hope she did.

Another patient in the ward had 3 cans of coke on her bed side table. Well, I couldn't let that go now could I. I told her that coke was used in the United States by the police to clean up road kill accident sites. She was a police officer herself by the way. I also told her that these fizzy drinks rob the body of calcium and make the bones weaker. It will dissolve anything you put in it. Put a coin in a glass of coke and you'll see what I mean. She asked what I drank instead. I told her that I juice. Making up healthy concoctions of apple, carrot, kale, celery and ginger or the like, or I just drank water with a little bit of organic elderflower cordial in it. Or I make smoothies. She said that she was going to treat herself to a juicer and a blender when she got out. I had been following a healthy diet for years now and I knew it was how I could manage my Lupus Disease better than most so I was always preaching to others about the importance of good nutrition. Your body deserves it.

As darkness fell the wind was picking up outside. I slept next to the window which was always open a few inches, no more. I think that the staff worried that if they were opened wider we would all be tying the sheets together and slipping out. How True!

The nurse had pulled the blinds but they were noisily flapping so I wedged a few of my personal items along the bottom. My shoes, my toilet bag, books etc. to hold the blind down. I was just dropping off to sleep when Crash Bang Wallop! Next thing I knew the crash team were by my bed `Deb are you alright` I looked up sheepishly `oops sorry` as they all realised what had happened. The whole ward was awake and laughing. `Let's try that again see if we can get a better time` shouts Jan. I must admit I'd never seen the staff move that quick before.

Tuesday 29th November.

Awoken at 6am to put nose bag on then went back to sleep for another couple of hours. I think I was getting a little more sleep now. Weight 53kg. I had been able to move my hips a little in bed last night to get comfortable. Hoorah I thought we`re getting some movement at last. The drugs must be kicking in.

Washed and managed to sip another glass of water. Sheer Nectar! We all take drinking water for granted but I can tell you I was savouring every single drop. Never again would I take water for granted.

One of the Pharmacists on the ward a marathon runner called `M` as he was known was told by the nurses that there was a fellow marathon runner on the ward. I think they're getting me mixed up with Paula Radcliff. He had come to say hello and saw my photos on my wall of Bob and I in our running gear. He recognised Bob and it transpired that Bob and M ran a similar pace and had probably seen each other at various events. We had chatted about various runs and he told me that he had just done the `Marathon des Sables`. Well for anyone who doesn't know. This is not just a marathon. It is what we call an `Ultra` Distances more than a 26.2 miler.

It is a 6 day ultra running event. Consisting of 156 miles, (251 km) run across the Sahara Desert in Morocco. Participants have to carry everything they need. Also apart from tents and water, they have to carry Food, clothing, medical supplies, sleeping bag etc. The temperatures can rise to 120F. It is considered the Toughest Foot Race on the Planet.

Needless to say us` mere runners` bow down to such individuals who are crazy enough to, not only attempt this insane adventure but to actually complete it in the allotted time, many don't. I had asked him to bring in his medal; I had always wanted to see one. I actually got to hold that medal and I had my photo taken. He must have thought that I'd lost my sanity while in here because he suggested that I give it a go. Yeah right! I told him that the mind might be willing but the body would not. I said as Clint Eastwood says `A man has to know his limitations`. I told him I was all up for a challenge but hey there is a line to be drawn here. `It was great to be chatting about running but I wasn't sure if I would ever get back to it. M assured me that I would. I hoped he was right.

Steve came to visit and we spent a couple of hours talking running. He had brought me a laminated running photo of Bob, me, Steve and Julie at the `Death Run` we`d done a few months previously. The run is a 12 mile cross country race in Devon through a hamlet that had been wiped out by the `Black Death` plague. The run is gorgeous with stunning scenery much of it being in the woods. The marshals all dress up as Grim Reapers, hooded and holding scythes to point the way. The winners are presented with a life size stone skull as their trophy. It`s great fun.

The photo Steve had brought me was of the four of us at the Finish Line where we are standing with one of the Grim Reapers, under a huge banner saying `Black Death. Welcome to Hell` How appropriate is that. It is` Hell` in here. We should put that same poster over my bed. We both laughed. Thanks Steve.

I do so love having visitors but it`s so difficult to talk after a while. My tongue feels as if it swells to twice its size and my facial muscles seem to seize up. So it was very tiring.

Just as Steve was leaving I was looking forward to a rest. That would have to wait as I had another visitor. It was Sandra a lovely lady from my falls prevention class. Sandra had been very good to me, always bringing me useful presents, hankies, notelets, hand cream and such like. Today she brought me a Scottish flag. `This is for you to carry at your first run back `she said. I told her that I would carry it across the finish line at the Edinburgh ½ Marathon in May. I had entered the full marathon but that would be a bit too much so the Half was my goal.

Julia arrived next with news of her 99th Marathon, yes you read it right. 99th. Julia is one of my inspirations. Julia is 63 years old and she has been running the same amount of years as I have. We met in our first year of running. I was always just behind her and now and again I would catch her up and we would exchange a few words before she would take off again leaving me in her trail. I have made many friends while running. Sport is wonderful for that.

Julia told me that her 100th marathon would be a home run. It was to be the Portsmouth Marathon in December. Bob was also going to be running that one. I would so like to be there to cheer them on and to watch Julia's face as she crossed that finish line of her 100th Marathon. But I would be stuck in here.

We were all interrupted when a porter came to take me for yet another scan. This was the breast ultra scan, so they could check out `the raisin` under my arm on my right breast. I donned my sunglasses and got into the wheelchair. The girls laughed at the glasses. I told them it was so bright down there I needed them. Sandra said I could do with a sun visor; she would bring me one on her next visit. I`ve got some really thoughtful friends.

I was wheeled into the room, stripped off to the waist and a gown placed across my boobs for decency, as I was laid on my back next to the scan screen. The two doctors then explained it all. The cold jelly, what they were looking for, they even showed me the screen. It is really weird to be looking at the inside of your body.

They told me that everything looked quite normal and did not think that my `raisin` was anything to worry about. Wow! Good news. That did lift my spirits somewhat I can tell you.

As I was being wheeled back to the ward Bob was coming in the door it was so good to see him and be able to give him some good news at last.

I wanted to spend some quiet time with Bob but as soon I was back in bed the nurse was around to do the `ob.'s` again. Eventually we were alone. Bob had brought me more cards and as I read them they brought tears to my eyes. It was really humbling to know that so many people out there were wishing me well and saying prayers for me. I had never realised how well I was thought of.

> `Good Friends are like Stars. You can`t always see them,
> but you know they`re always there`

Again when it was time for Bob to go I went into the patients lounge, sat in the dark and sobbed my heart out. `This is not my life`

Wednesday 30th November

Good sleep apart from the usual 3 am wake up with dry mouth and throat. Showered and had a big break through this morning. The doc was doing his rounds and when he got to me I was grinning like a Cheshire cat. `How are you this morning ` `Well doc, it may not mean much to you being a man and all but I managed to shave my legs this morning? The Gorilla look has gone! ` He burst out laughing. I don`t think he had expected that for an answer. Although no one had been able to see my gorilla legs because I always had to wear the Paula Radcliffe's as I called them, the D.V.T white socks. He then told me that my scan from yesterday was `all clear`

Yippee another hill climbed. He also said that the next step for me was rehab. I stressed my concern. I thought rehab was for when you were nearly fixed up as it were. I felt far from it! The good thing about rehab was that it would be home in Portsmouth. The hospital was right next door to Bob`s work so I would be able to see him every day. What Joy. I still had the P.E.T scan to have and that would be here in Southampton so I wasn`t going anywhere yet.

This was the one I was really worried about. It`s the biggie. The scanner looks at cellular level. Where the other scanners may have missed something this monster would find it wherever, it was hiding.

Dr B and whole team came to see me. They did various tests and said they could see definite improvements in my strength. What really lifted my spirit though was Dr B said that I would be home for Christmas. Yippee! Although the way I feel at the moment it is hard to believe. Maybe she means next Christmas?

I can`t wait to go home. The very thought of being in my own home again and snuggling up to Bob in our own bed. Walking along the beach and getting as much fresh air as I want. It can't come quickly enough.

I told the docs that I wanted some information on this LEMS .I told them `I'm a tough cookie but I need to know what it is I'm fighting`. Again they didn't appear too keen to oblige. Looks passed between them all that did give me cause for concern. (Weeks later once I was out of hospital I went to the library to look it all up. I knew then why they had all been so reluctant) It makes for grim reading. Mind you I thought there is nothing about the 20% of us who have the auto-immune type of LEMS. It's all about the 80%, usually smokers who will have an underlying cancer which usually appears within 2 years. There is a definite need for more or should I say any information for the minority group here. Perhaps I could suggest to my doctors that I put one together. If I can help anyone else out there who has to go through this awful ordeal it would be a good thing.

The reason I am writing this book is to help others with lupus and LEMS to see that auto-immune disease is not the end of the world. It is so easy to give in to disease. I`ve seen it. However there is hope after diagnosis. If you are willing to fight back for your life, you can do it! It would give me enormous pleasure to think that my story could inspire others to put up a fight and just watch as they come out on top.

I also told the doctors that when I got back running I would send them a picture of me with my medal at the finish. Again that look passed between them all. I knew what they were thinking. You just wait and see I thought.

I told them with a glint in my eye. `I`ve been here before, with my Lupus. I had managed to tame my wolf. I would do the same with the LEMS, you`ll see. `

After they had left I remembered another occasion I had had that glint in my eye.

One day a few summers ago in 2006 Bob and I were leaving the house to cycle down to the beach for a swim. I was holding my bike ready to go when it fell over caught my leg in the pedal and I promptly fell on top of it. The side of the pedal went straight through the side of my knee cap. I won`t repeat the expletives but suffice to say it bloody well hurt.

Bob dashed in doors to get something to stop the bleeding, the neighbours came running over with a blanket and a cushion and Bob came out with a dirty dishtowel. If I hadn't been in such pain I would've laughed. Men.

Anyway I'm at A&E being stitched up and I say to the doc, `When can I run again` He looks at me `Ooh It`ll be a while` `But I've got the South of England fell Running Championships on the isle of Wight at the end of next week` `Well, I'm afraid you won`t be doing those` he replied. If he had been looking at my face instead of watching his sutures he would have seen `that glint` in my eye.

A week later when we are on the Isle of Wight having a week`s holiday before the race weekend. I am at the village GP practice on the Tuesday morning to have my stitches out and I ask the nurse the same question also I ask` when can I sea swim.` She replies `A couple of weeks ` to both.

Fifteen minutes later, I am in the sea enjoying a swim. It was wonderful.

The weekend arrives. Saturday morning I do the 3 mile race. Felt fine. Saturday afternoon I do the 8 mile race. I felt elated. Sunday morning I do the Half Marathon. They are all tough hilly but beautifully scenic runs and I loved every moment of them.

As usual I was last in all 3 races, so you can imagine my shock when I am sat eating my lunch at the prize giving ceremony to hear them call out my name for the silver medal for my age category. I thought nay they must have that wrong, but no, it was mine. You see there had only been 2 of us girls in the 45+ age group who did all 3 races. How amazing is that?

The forward in the book by Oscar Pretorius (Blade Runner) written by his mother says that

` A loser is not one who runs last in a race, It is the one who sits and watches, and never tries to run` How True.

You should`ve seen the Glint in my eye as I walked up to be presented with my medal. If only that Doctor and nurse had seen me they`d have had a fit.

`I can take a licking` but I`ll keep on kicking`

December 1st

My hips definitely feel stronger today. I can actually roll up to sitting from prone in bed wow! The drugs are kicking in at last. My weight is still dropping. 51.9kg. Wish I could get a Kit Kat up this tube.

Bob and Gary have cycled in to see me today it took them 2 ½ hours. We went down to the canteen, me walking in between them holding an arm either side for support. I felt a right old biddy. Bob went to get tea. He seemed to be away ages. All I wanted was to be held. I was missing him so much it hurt. I wished he had sent Gary for the tea and we could've had a few moments together. We all sat outside in the crisp fresh air and chatted. Unfortunately they couldn't stay long as they wanted to get home before it got dark. The A27 is notoriously busy and dangerous in daylight; if possible people avoid cycling on it in the dark. Just as they were about to leave the heavens opened up and it began to pour down. They were in for an extremely wet ride home. What I'd have given to be going with them. I saw them off and went again into the patients lounge for a good cry. `This is not my life`

December 2nd

Dr Ash and another doctor that I've not seen before are doing the rounds. This new doctor says to me `Do you know what the P.E.T scan is for` Yes it's to look for cancer. ` He looked at me as if he knew that the scan would find it. After they left I broke down in tears, I couldn`t stop. I couldn't stop thinking about `chemo` and what I might have to go through. I know it sounds dramatic and anyone who knows me will say that it's not like me to give in, but no one knows how hard I've had to fight all these years to keep myself well. It takes real commitment to stick to a very strict regime. Jan heard my sobs and came over to embrace me in a big bear hug.

Later I asked the nurse to show me how to do the NG caper so that I could manage it all by myself. I had to take back some of the control of my life, and as they couldn't tell me how long I would have this in for the sooner I learnt the better. Plus I could then put in whatever I liked, my wheatgrass, my vitamin powders, as much water as I wanted. No one would know.

The specialist nurse came for another chat to ask if I had any concerns. Any concerns. How long can you stay? I thought. Am I going to be able to lead a normal life again? Am I going to need a stair lift put in? Will I be able to work? Will I always have to be fed through my nose? I told her that I felt so helpless and depressed as no one could give me any information. I have nothing to work with here. I have no idea what is going to happen to me.

There was another panic attack for the nurse doing the `obs` today when the machine shows I am flat lining. `You`re dead` she says. `Why is it that none of our machines work with you but every other patient they are fine? It`s weird` she exclaimed.

December 3rd

Another patient had some bad news today. Josephine had come in for tests; she thought she had simply pulled a muscle. She had been pushing her daughter around in a wheelchair, her daughter had broken her leg skiing. Her right arm had been very stiff and painful. However the doctor suspected something a lot more sinister. I heard the doc ask her when her family would next be in. I knew from the last few weeks in hospital that when you are asked that question it is serious. It was. Josephine and her family were told she had Motor Neurone Disease. They were also told she had 6 -18 months to live. Josephine was only 63 years old. What made it so much of a shock was that although the disease was so advanced she had had no warning at all. Josephine had felt well up until now.

After the meeting Josephine came back to the ward, pulled the curtain around her bed and sobbed. I left her a while and then popped my head around the curtain. `Do you need a hug` I asked? She nodded. I sat on her bed with my arm around her and she told me the whole story. I was devastated.

Josephine turned out to be an extraordinary person. After she had had a good cry on my shoulder, she seemed to be taking it all in her stride and spoke in a very matter of fact way. She wanted to have one last holiday in Easter at her holiday home in France. We also spoke about how her husband and she had already spoken about funerals and the music they wanted as he had been living on borrowed time with cancer for years now. They had always assumed that he would be the first to go. I laughed when she told me he wanted a Johnny Cash song for his cremation. I joked `Not Ring of Fire` she laughed `no, a boy named Sue`

I then joked` well at least you`ll be able to eat whatever you like` Josephine said she could murder a bar of chocolate right now. `what`s your favourite` I asked` Lindt dark` she replied. I disappeared through her curtain and promptly returned with just such a bar in my hand. I just happened to have one in my locker which Helen my friend had brought me on day 2 of my hospitalization which I had been saving for when I could eat again. Josephine's eyes lit up. The look on her tear stained face was   priceless. I gave her the bar. It was unwrapped in a second. I swear it didn`t touch the sides. I`d never seen anyone eat a bar of chocolate that quickly or seen such a look of sheer delight after it was gone. I told Josephine that if it were me I would eat chocolate cake every day. She was looking forward to some wine. She would drink wine every day. The next few days were to prove to me how strong the human spirit can be. Josephine's grace and calmness and warm spirit shone through like a beacon of light to everyone on the ward. Having her here with us helped us all enormously cope with our own problems.

We would chat about all sorts of things. Who would we like to meet who has passed on before us? We both agreed on Danny Kaye. I suppose we were showing our age as the other girls in the ward being younger in their 20`s didn't know who he was. Vicky one of the younger patients looked him up on her flashy phone. She got Danny Kaye and Louis Armstrong on you tube singing` when the saints come marching in. `

The volume went up and there we all were singing along to this well-known tune. We were in Southampton Hospital and this song was Southampton Football clubs anthem. The nurse`s were all popping in to see what was going on. I think the nurses thought we`d slipped in some booze. It was so funny.

Sadly Josephine did not make her Easter Holiday to France. She passed away only 3 months later at home with all her family around her. I will never forget her. I hope where ever she is now that they have a good supply of dark chocolate and good wine.

`Death leaves a Heartache no one can heal.

Love leaves a memory no one can steal. `

I think what we need in hospital is an `official hugger` someone to come around and give out hugs to anyone who needs one. I thought that perhaps in a big cute bear suit. In fact, a few years ago I had wanted to do just that. I wanted to hire a Winnie the Pooh suit and go up to the hospital at Christmas time and go around the wards giving hugs. Of course you can imagine the response from the hospital administrator. In this `nanny state` we have now such a thing would not be possible. I thought what a Shame. What sort of a world are we living in?

In one of my Tai Chi classes we do have an `Official Hugger` his name is Les. He stands at the door as they all come in. Anyone who wants or needs a hug gets one. His wife Anne is there too she doesn't mind at all. As most of the 50 -60 people in my class are over 50 many of them are single or don't have family around and don't get many hugs. I always jokingly tell my classes that you need 6 hugs a day for good health. Grab anybody, the Postman, the Dustman, lollypop lady or the Traffic warden just before he puts a ticket on your windscreen. It always gets a good laugh.

December 4th

I didn't sleep much at all last night. Couldn't stop thinking about my friend Josephine.

 When Dr S came around to ask how I was I had more good news for him. `Well doc, not only did I shower myself this morning but I actually managed to shave under my arms. The hedgehogs have gone. He threw his head back and laughed.

When Bob arrived we went outside for some fresh air. It felt so good to be out together. On the way back to the lift I turned to the stairs behind me and told Bob I wanted to try a few steps. He held my hand and I held onto the bannister with the other. I felt very nervous. I tentatively lifted my leg up onto the first step and felt it was almost impossible. I felt so weak. In the back of my mind I was thinking of the 13 steps we have at home. If I can't climb up one step how was I going to manage at home with 13?

Coming out of the lift we met Dr S. Bob asked him how I was progressing. Doc said that I must think of it as a Marathon not a sprint. Good analogy doc. I`ve never sprinted in my life but I've done a few marathons. He then joked about the mass of cards I now had strung up on string around my bed. `If you get any more, the ward walls are going to be pulled down with the weight of them all`

Bob also brought me news that the Olympic Torch bearers had been announced. I had been short listed but as I had not been informed I knew now that I was `bombed out`. What a pity. That would really have spurred me on to get fit and well again. It is amazing how you can heal when you have something to aim for.

I remember years ago when we were working and living in at Denham Golf Club. There was an airfield right next door and Bob had booked me a flying lesson for my birthday. I was very excited. However, just about 2 weeks before my birthday treat I was diagnosed with a very bad case of

Shingles. The Doctor told me I would take several weeks to get better. I was in a lot of pain and felt absolutely drained. However by the time my big day came around I was right as rain. I was raring to go. It was a clear case of `The Body will follow the heart and Mind` I was not going to miss my lesson.

Bob was supposed to be running the Santa 10km today .An event we should have been doing together. It`s great fun. Hundreds of people all dressed in Santa suits either walking or running along our seafront. Some people even dress their dogs up as Santa. He didn't want to do it without me and besides he wanted to spend the day with me here.

We were lying on my bed now and I was showing him all the gadgets. How, at the touch of a button I could raise or lower, fold in half or raise one end of the bed. He was like a kid with a new toy. Going up Menswear! One of the other girls in the ward had her 2 young boys visiting and they too joined in the fun, making their mums bed rise and fold like a sandwich almost squashing them all. We all laughed together. You don't get much reason to laugh in here and it felt good. God I've got to get out of here. The phrase `Don`t let the Bastards grind you down ` comes to mind a lot in here.

`This is not my life`

The doctors all came to tell me that they would be sending me to `Phoenix Ward ` Q.A Portsmouth next week after I had my P.E.T Scan. I said `Phoenix eh, risen from the dead, how appropriate 'They all laughed.

Dr D again said to the others how special I was. I don't want to be special I just want to be normal!

It may seem a bit trivial to many, but my hair was in dire need of some attention. I needed a cut and colour desperately. The fact that I had been unable to wash and blow dry it for weeks now was getting me down. I had always prided myself on my appearance. Anita had in fact on a couple of occasions now called me a scarecrow. Thanks Anita just wait until I get out of here girl. You can always trust a good friend to tell you the truth about yourself.

Monday December 5th

I asked the pharmacist if I could have my own pill crusher. Although I was now doing my own NG tube, I still had to rely on a nurse bringing me a crusher before I could administer my meds. This had been proving a problem and consequently I had been putting them in much later on occasion than I was supposed to.

In the afternoon, the sister came to ask if I would mind being on television. Meridian Tonight our local news channel was going to do a piece on one of our volunteers `Carla`, she was being given a 50years service award. I asked `When? ` `Now` she replied. Blimey no time to spruce myself up then and me with yet another bad hair day. `O.K bring it on`

Carla was to fuss around my bed tidying up my table and plumping my pillows while being filmed. Carla was a really bubbly 80 year old retired nurse who had worked on this very ward. She was always singing as she worked and her favourite was Tom Jones.

Picture the scene if you will. Me propped up in bed looking like I had been dragged through a hedge backwards. Carla singing `sex bomb, sex bomb you're my little sex bomb as she fussed around me. I was in hysterics. Sex bomb I look like shit!!!! The camera man was really having fun. The interviewer could hardly get his words out he was laughing so much. Wiggle your hips Carla he`s saying. All the staff had come to watch and everybody was laughing. Tears were running down my face and for once they were tears of joy.

This was going out on the 6`oclock news tonight. Wait until I tell Bob. He`ll love this.

I phoned Bob to tell him. He had no idea how to work the recorder so would ask Julie and Pete to tape it for me.

Later that night I went to watch it in the patients lounge.

The tiny patients lounge seats about 3 -4 people at a squeeze. The television is up on a wall bracket at about head height and there is no remote control for it. How was I going to manage to reach up to turn it on I thought. There was no way that I could lift my arms up to do it. Bob always calls me his logical babe, and I guess he`s right. I will look for a way. I found it. I leaned in to the television and pressed the on switch with my nose, low and behold it came on and it was on the channel that I wanted. I chuckled and gently lowered myself into a chair. The local news came on and there I was.   My God I looked so ill but hey I was still laughing.

Tuesday 6th December

I had a wonderful dream last night. I was running free along a mountain top with a 360°views all around me. I was wearing a long white loose fitting garment, the sort you see the ancient Greeks wearing. My hair and my dress were flowing out behind me as I ran. I was smiling.

I then came to a high wire fence where there was a crowd of people all trying to climb over to freedom on the other side. I turned to my right and there smiling at me was George `bloody` Clooney. He plants a kiss on my cheek and lifts me up and over the fence. Once I am over the other side I`m off running again.

Hey Girls, You all want to know what it was I ate to give me such a dream. Well. Trust me you wouldn`t want to have this stuff I have going up through my snout, even for a kiss from George.

I awoke with a very dry throat and my mouth felt like sandpaper. Well I had run a few miles hadn`t I?

Even after such a lovely dream I felt depressed. I felt like a caged animal and I just wanted out of here. I miss the outdoors, my running, cycling walking with the wind in my hair being out in nature. It doesn't take a psychologist to analyse my dream. The fence is the hospital as for George – well girls need I say more?

Normally I am a` glass half full` kind of girl but these past few weeks have been wearing me down. Being surrounded by ill people and even knowing and witnessing that some of the poor souls will die in here has a very negative effect on me. I`ve always been a sensitive type and the atmosphere in here was draining my energies. I also found that whenever I had visitors, Bob or friends I could not show them how frightened I was. I would always put on an act for them and bottle it all up inside. However when they had all gone all the emotions would come to the surface and I would take refuge in the patients lounge and cry my eyes out. I had to get out of here.

Wednesday 7th December

I had friends visiting today. I just wish I didn't get so tired .Talking for any length of time was impossible. If you knew me you would know that talking is usually no problem at all.

A lot of the staff have been jokingly asking for my autograph after seeing me on the news last night.

 Yippee. Gareth one of the physiotherapists comes to say they are going to try me on some exercises. Now you're talking! Bring it on. Bob came along too.

Down in the Neuro Gym I try a few squats holding onto the parallel bars. We tried throwing and catching a ball, I then had a go on a wobble board and that was me exhausted. I could see that Bob was amazed how hard these exercises were for me to do. I found this all hard to accept, me, a keep fit teacher and yet I feel knackered after doing so little, but hey it was a start ,but I knew it was going to be a long journey back to fitness.

I had always found that I felt better after exercise and although I felt tired I felt elated that I had finally after all these weeks of inactivity made a start. `Exercise to Energise 'To be the pupil instead of the teacher was also very strange for me.

Later that evening Dr Ash came to say goodbye he was moving on to his next posting. Before he went I said I would like a picture of him and Josephine and Lord Lamby (that was Josephine's cuddly toy her hubby had brought her in for comfort and cuddles) the nurses had put a wrist identification tag on it and I asked the doc if he would check out Lord Lambys heart with his stethoscope for a photo. I wanted to send Josephine a copy of it once she got home. It was a lovely picture they were both laughing as the doc leaned over them both for their examination. I am sure now with Josephine gone that her family will treasure that photo. I know that I will always remember that scene. In fact I still keep a copy of that picture on my wall.

Bob had told me today how much he was missing me. He said that he would hate to live without me. He hated coming home to an empty home. He also hated not having me to snuggle up to at night. Maybe I should buy him a Lord Lamby. I too hated being without him. What worried me though was if they do find cancer and I don't pull through who will look after him? Please God. Don't let them find any.

Once again as soon as he left I was crying and rocking myself in the patients lounge. I hate this NG tube. My nose is running with the crying and I can't even blow it. When the damn thing comes out I am going to eat a whole box of mince pies.

Thursday 8th December

Pretty good sleep last night. Now I am doing my own aspiration I can get as much water down me during the day and find that I don't wake up in the early hours feeling like I've been wandering around the desert for days looking for a water hole. It feels good to take control of a bit of my life again. I am now sneaking in my vitamin powders and wheatgrass juice without having to lie to the nurses. Today I would start my own exercise programme.

I started with 3 walks up and down the corridor. Of course Fred had to come along too.10 squats, 10 leg swings, 10 one legged knee bends and 10 abductor/adductor swings.

Dr B decided that now I was more mobile I did not need the Alendronate (bone protector).Great I thought one less drug to take. She also wanted to try a few days without the 3, 4- Dap to see what happened. The P.C.T would not approve such an expensive drug without proof that I did definitely need it as the drug apparently didn't work for everyone. At £60,000 a pop I could understand why.

The machines are still playing up with me. My lung function test reads 9.99 ha-ha I don't think so. The highest reading apparently would be 7 so I was way over the top. Maybe with a lung capacity like that I was ready for my next marathon or hey how about the Marathon Des Sables?

Nurse put in another cannula. This was for the P.E.T scan tomorrow. Oh God! I had yet more blood taken too. Crikey what are they doing with it all? I managed two fruit purees today. My swallow must be improving?

There is to be a carol concert tonight down in the foyer. The sister asked if anyone wanted to go. I love Christmas music and jumped at the chance. I wandered down there at 6pm in my pyjamas and dressing gown. It was too cold to go outside so the doors were left open so the patients could sit inside. They were serving mulled wine and mince pies, the aroma was mouth-watering all I could do was look on with envy as everyone scoffed away. Not for the first time I cursed this damn tube.

The singing started and I found myself miming the words. I couldn't sing. My throat would not make the sounds. Of course I thought the muscles are not working. Talking as I knew was difficult but singing was impossible. I started to feel very sorry for myself. Bob and I usually go to a few carol concerts and stand hand in hand singing together. I miss him so much it hurts. I wondered if I really would get home for Christmas. After the concert I slowly wandered back to the ward put on my earphones and listened to my Christmas choral music C.D's. The tears started to stream down my face.

Friday 9th December

I had been sleeping really well but I was awoken at 5a.m by nurses wrapping up Christmas presents. How would they like it if we all turned up in their bedroom to do the same? It's incredible isn't it?

No nosebag this morning I've got my P.E.T Scan today at 12noon. Ugh! I`m hungry and everyone else is tucking into their breakfast. Torture!

My head is feeling very heavy today and I'm finding it hard to hold up. I wonder if it`s because I'm doing without the 3, 4- Dap?

The P.E.T Scan! This is the one I fear the most. If there is even a tiniest spot of cancer in my body this scan will seek it out. I'm terrified. Knowing that my father died of cancer when he was not much older than I am only adds to the terror.

A nurse comes to take me down to B level and outside to the mobile unit in the car park. It`s been raining and the ground is wet. My feet get soaked through my thin slippers and are very cold as I tentatively haul myself up the 7 metal steps using the handrails. I am terrified of slipping, I can`t afford a fall. I am shown into a small room, quite cosy, carpeted with a small couch, desk and chair. The only décor in the room is a beautiful picture of a single bright orange flower, vibrant against the clinical cream coloured walls. A nurse sits at the desk and begins to explain the procedure to me. I then have to sign a consent form before I am taken into what I can only describe as a space capsule. Through a glass wall I can see a huge control panel with 3 people working at it. It looks like the bridge on the Star ship Enterprise. I expected Captain Kirk`s voice to say `Take her to warp speed Mr Spock`

Another nurse takes over. The pod we are in there is barely room to swing a cat. The nurse shoots saline up into my cannula to check its working properly. The nurse then shows me into a long thin room with a sun lounger in it. Next she appears with a small metal container about the size of a demi- tasse. This contains the radioactive dye which will help to show up any cancerous cells clearly. It`s quite comical as the nurse standing as far away from me as her arm length allows injects the liquid into my cannula. I am then wrapped in a blanket and I put on my earphones to listen to Classic FM while I let the liquid permeate my whole body which I am told will take a full hour.

I think I must have dropped off because the hour seemed to go by ever so quickly. I heard a disembodied voice ask if I am alright and asking me to step through the door. Just as I'm looking for one the whole wall slides open. (I am on the Enterprise) There sits the scanner. It looks just like another gigantic ring donut.

I`m told to take off all jewellery and place it all in a tray by the table. Just like at the airport. I am laid on the sliding table and my arms are put into a sort of straight jacket and laid across my belly. A big cushion is slid under my legs for comfort and the nurse leaves the room. As the big wall panel closes I feel very much alone and very scared.

I close my eyes and feel the table start to lift and slide into the donut. It is very noisy but not unpleasant. I had been panicking when I'd heard that I had to have all these scans as the thought of the sealed capsule I'd seen on TV terrified me, I don't like enclosed spaces. This donut however was fine as I could see all around me.

The 20 minutes passed quite quickly and before I knew it the panel slides open and the nurse standing in the doorway tells me I can get up. Well easy for her to say. I tell her `I can`t I'm afraid my muscles aren't working` This is when the comedy sketch ensued. `I will throw you a rope with knots in it, grab hold of one and I'll haul you up` I thought she's kidding right. She wasn't. Of course as I am now radioactive no one should come close to me. The rope was about the thickness of a broom handle the knots all along the rope where the size of bloody oranges. I thought if one of those buggers hits me on the head they won`t need to worry about the scan results they'll be organizing my funeral instead. I thought where`s Jeremy Beadle?

The nurse suddenly turns into John Wayne as she lassos the rope around her head and throws it with great accuracy towards me. I`m almost disappointed when I don`t hear her holler `Yeehaaa` I grab hold of it, fumble for an orange and hold tight. It feels like I`m in a `tug of war` The nurse says `Good Catch, 1,2,3, up you come` I must've looked like a mummy rising from the dead. I must admit though the whole procedure did make me laugh. Wait until I tell Bob about this little caper.

I was told that I would be radioactive for the next 4 hours and that no one was allowed within 4 metres of me. Also if I went to the loo I had to `double flush 'Do you remember the `Ready Break` advert? Well I had the Glow.

` This is life Jim, but not as we know it` Doctor McCoy says to Captain Kirk.

As I was walked back to the ward I was joking with everybody `Unclean, unclean, keep your distance, coming through 'The whole ward wanted to hear all about it. And we were all soon in fits of laughter.

Shortly after I got back one of my friends from Tai Chi class Kath came to visit. As she turned into the ward and saw me she made a beeline for me with her arms open wide to embrace me in a huge bear hug. I warned her I was radioactive to which her reply was `bugger that` and hugged me anyway. We both burst into tears as she told me she thought I would look a lot worse. I assured her I was ok. We had a lovely chat and she told me that all my class members were missing me and wishing me a speedy recovery.

Later that day Gareth and Mat the physiotherapists came along and they had brought an exercise bike with them for me to try. Now you`re talking I thought. Deciding I was ok with that they then took me to the stairwell to try a few steps. They wanted me to try to do one step up and two back.

With one of them on my side and the other behind me I took hold of the rail. As I tried to lift my leg up it felt so heavy and stiff it felt impossible I suddenly recalled a fantastic movie I'd watched recently about the true story of Carl Brashear. (Played by Cuba Gooding Jnr)

In the 1950`s and 1960`s racial prejudice was still rife in the United States especially in the U.S Navy. If you were black the only jobs offered to you were that of a cook.

Carl Brashear was determined to be more than just a cook. He had always loved the water and he believed that he was born for the job of navy diver. He fought against all the odds and he made it, he became a navy diver, only to lose a leg a few years later saving another sailors life. The hierarchy try to use his disability against him to get rid of him. He persuades them to give him 3 months with his prosthetic leg to get himself fit enough to re- take the physical examination which will be reviewed by the navy medical board.

He works hard and within the allotted time he is back to full physical fitness. The day arrives and he must prove that he can walk 12 paces unaided in full diving rig. In those days the suit weighed a ton, 290lb in actual fact (20 stone). First, there was the huge round copper helmet, the weighted boots and then the suit itself was extremely heavy and cumbersome not like the neoprene light weight suits they wear today.

At the test, in front of the whole governing Navy Board Carl has the help of his old adversary who had since come to respect and admire Carl. Master Chief Sunday (played by Robert De Niro) As Carl struggles to his feet from a sitting position Chief Sunday shouts `Sailor, square that rig` Carl manages to stand up. He then has to take his 12 unaided steps up to the line to complete his task. After the first 4 steps Sunday see`s that Carl is struggling and he hollers at him. `Come on Cookie I want my 12! A navy man is not a fighting man he is a salvage expert. If it's lost, he finds it, if its sunk, he brings it up, if it's in his way, he moves it, if he`s lucky he will die young 200′ beneath the waves, because that is the closest he will ever get to being a hero, hell I don`t know why anyone would want to be a navy diver`. It is a fabulous film. Of course Carl does it but you can see on his face what it took him to do it.

`All it takes is all you`ve got`

The super thing about the DVD is that the special features include real footage of the man himself and you see him as he is now. It is such an inspirational story.

In 1968 Carl Brashear became the 1st amputee in U.S Naval history to return to full, active duty. Two years later, he became a Master Diver. He did not retire from the navy for another 9 years.

Now I could imagine that same look on my face as I struggled to do my task. I now imagined Robert De Niro barking at me `Come on Debbie I want my 12`. If you haven't seen the film by the way it's truly inspirational stuff, go get it and see. You won`t be disappointed. `Men of Honour`

I managed very slowly with the encouragement and patience of the lads to walk up two flights of stairs. I felt elated but knackered and I was actually sweating it had taken so much effort but I'd done it. Carl Brashear, I am sure, would be proud of me.

At the end of the film there is a song written and performed by Brian McKnight titled `Win`. The words are fabulous and really summed up my feelings.

Dark is the night, I can weather the storm.
At first say die, I`ve been down this road before.
I`ll never quit, I`ll never lay down.
You see I promised myself that I`d never let me down. So
I`ll never give up, never give in,
Never let a ray of doubt set in and if I fall, I`ll never feel, I`ll just get up and try again.
Never lose hope, never lose faith,
there`s much too much at stake.
Upon myself I must depend.
I`m not looking for place or show, I`m gonna win.

No stopping now, there`s still a ways to go.
Someway, somehow, whatever it takes I know.
I`ll never quit, I`ll never go down.
When it`s all said and done.
I`m gonna win.

My favourite books are inspirational stories. Over the years I have read many. They give me hope and spur me on to be all I can be. I`ve read Jane Tomlinson`s book about her fight against cancer and her amazing achievements. Just before coming in to hospital I had read Kate Allatt`s story of how she had fought back from a massive stroke (locked in syndrome) While I have been in hospital I have been reading Oscar Pretorius's (the fastest man on no legs) book. All of them are truly inspirational people.

 That song was going through my mind as the lads walked me back to my bed I was grinning from ear to ear at my achievement and yes the odd tear was starting to trickle down my face. 'Don't cry` the sister says as she is walking towards me `I've got good news. We`ve got you a bed in Portsmouth you`re off to rehab tomorrow` Yippee I`m on my way home to `Phoenix` I've risen from the dead. Now let's see what they can do for me. I had been told that I would get about 3 physiotherapy sessions a day there. And hey, I`ll get to see Bob every day. Yippee!!!!

The only thing that worried me was that everybody will want to visit, all my friends and all my class members. I regularly taught about 200 people a week. I couldn't cope with so many visitors as I wanted to concentrate all my energies into my exercise and get back to fitness as soon as I possibly could. I was determined to get home for Christmas.

I was also so looking forward to the journey. To see something of the outside world instead of the same view I'd had from my hospital bed for the past 4 ½ weeks.

Saturday 10th December

See something of the outside world? No Chance. I was taken to Q.A Hospital in an ambulance with frosted windows; I couldn't see a damn thing. I wished I could've sat up the front with the driver. I felt as if I was on a prison transfer.

When we got to Portsmouth I was deposited into Phoenix ward. Shortly after my arrival the doctor came around to see me and to put me back on the 3, 4- Dap. It was obvious that I did need that drug as I had reverted back to my ragdoll state during the few days without it.

Bob, Gary and Helen had all cycled up to welcome me home. It was so good to see them. Although I still felt awful and very unwell. I had assumed that by the time I got to rehab I would be on the mend, however I felt far from it and I wondered just how long I would be in here.

As we were chatting one of the physiotherapists came in to introduce himself. His name was Fungus Addams as in the Addams Family. (He had apparently changed his name by Deed pole.) He was 6foot tall, slim and had tattoos and piercings over all the parts of his body that I could see. I thought Blimey, What have we got here? He strolled up towards my bed rubbing his big hands together and said `Deborah, normally I have to drag patients into the gym for exercise, but I've been reliably informed (Anita) that I am going to have to drag you out` he grinned.

First he wanted to check what my mobility was like walking with `Fred` As I tried to walk towards the door Fred was going around in circles and I had to follow. It was worse than a Tesco trolley. I felt like a dog chasing its tail. Fungus found me another tripod and we tried again, this one wouldn't move at all. Maybe I should stick with the first one at least I would get a lot of exercise, a bit like a hamster running in his wheel. Third time lucky we found a Fred who could dance and we were off along the corridor to see the gym. This was going to be my saviour. I could come in here whenever I liked. Yippee!

Back on the ward the nurses all introduced themselves and they knew about my intolerance to bright lights. They said that the lights are not required during the day as the ward was so bright. In fact one whole side of the ward was a huge window which had a fabulous view out over Cosham Hill. A vast green area I knew well which was great for walking especially on blustery autumn days such as these. I would gaze up at the hill and long to be out there. One downside to the view though was that if I looked down from my 3rd floor window I looked straight onto the Mortuary! Are they trying to tell me something? That was about the only department that I hadn't been seen by and I was going to keep it that way!

The transfer and all the visits had tired me out and I just wanted to do my drugs and get some rest.

Doing my drugs was like a scene from an Alchemists workshop. I`d sit on the side of my bed, pull up my wee table. On the table were all my drugs which the nurse had dished out and placed into separate tiny paper cups. I then had to crush each drug separately put it into a cup of water and then syringe it up my tube. There were 7 different drugs to be done. The whole procedure took me about 35 minutes. I felt like Harry Potter, maybe I could magic my way out of here?

Sunday 11th December

I slept great! It is so much quieter in here. I took a long walk with Fred along the corridor. It was hard work but I felt I had achieved something although I had a feeling of wanting to be sick. I found out later that it was the feed. Different hospitals use different feed bags. Great! Here we go again. It took another 2 days for my poor stomach to get used to the new feed. I was up and running if you get my drift? Not for the first time I thought just let me die.

Thankfully those thoughts did not last long. Just as I was feeling sorry for myself in walks Bob and Anita. They had some great news for me. Anita had persuaded the Sister to allow me out for a day to watch the marathon! She had told the Sister that she would be with me the whole time and would look after me. I was overjoyed! Not only would I be able to see Bob do his run but I would be there to watch Julia as she crossed the line of her 100th marathon. How fantastic is that. We decided to keep it a secret from her and surprise her on the big day. I couldn't wait to see the expression on her face when she saw me at the finish line. Julia would become a member of a very elite running club called the `100 Marathon Club`

Thinking about names of running clubs there is a club called the `Coffin Dodgers` I wonder if they'll let me in?

 Anita was to pop in to see me every day while I was in there after she finished work. She would always be able to make me laugh.

Monday 12th December

I slept right through the night! How wonderful is that? Shower, Harry Potter, doctors rounds, dietician (my feed is now being increased to 1750kc a day) The occupational therapist came to assess me too. Things were happening!

Fungus came to get me for my first session of the day. He was a great character. Warm and friendly and very encouraging, everybody loved him. As we were walking along to the gym Bob and Gary arrived so Fungus asked them to come along too.

It really upset me to see just how weak I was and I knew more than most just what it was going to take to get back to any kind of fitness level. The lads couldn't believe how hard I was working to do what would normally for me be very easy exercises. Although when I look back I have done it all before so I can do it again. Bob and Gary both looked very concerned. Poor Bob also looked very tired. These past few weeks had put a real strain on him.

Later, Anita had popped in after work for our daily chat. I was talking so much that my mouth filled up with saliva that I couldn't swallow and consequently I was choking again. I started to panic. Anita ran for the nurse but I knew I couldn't wait, I was thinking of the Mortuary below my window so I pulled the tube out and miraculously my breathing returned to normal phew! That was a close one. My relief was soon forgotten as I realised that another tube would have to go in tonight as I still had my drugs to put in.

After Anita left, the Sister came to put in another NG tube. Another nurse held my hand and the Sister began feeding the tube up my nose and over the bridge down into my throat. It didn't want to play ball and I tried very hard to relax and eventually it was in. Now all that had to be done was to pull out the wire. It wouldn't come out. The Sister was tugging and tugging. I expected her to put her knee on my chest to get a better grip it was like a tug` o` war going on. I could see how hard the sister was pulling as she was sweating and turning rather red. Eventually it was out, but the damn tube had split so another one would have to be put in. By this time I was in tears. I had had enough. It was all so painfully uncomfortable and exhausting. I just wanted to go to sleep and not wake up again. The Sister decided to leave me to rest for a few hours and the she would try again later. This was to turn out a blessing. `This is not my life`

Later that night nurse Emma came to put in my NG. `I heard you had a bad time earlier Debs? Don't you worry I am very good at doing these and I promise you will have it in in no time` She was as good as her word and before I knew it I had my tube in place. Emma told me that during her training she had volunteered herself to be a guinea pig for the other nurses to train in this procedure so she knew exactly what it felt like to have an NG Tube put in. Emma then put my drugs in for me as she could see I was exhausted. Knowing that having had to take my drugs so late the steroids would keep me awake for hours she suggested I borrow one of the portable DVD players that are available on the ward. These had been donated by the` Friends of the hospital` a group of volunteers who ran a café and shop to raise funds for the patients. I was over the moon. Movies! I love my films. Emma brought me round a selection of 6 DVD`s one of which was the Sound of Music. I was in my element. On it went and I lay back in bed with my headphones on and lost myself in Austria for 2 ½ hours. I lay there silently singing along to all the songs. It was sheer bliss. Watching a movie certainly beat crying myself to sleep.

I was the happiest I'd been in the last 5 weeks. I love movies and from that night on I would look forward to settling down at night to be transported to another world and then I would fall into a happy blissful sleep.

I must remember when I get out of here to pop along to the Friends Café and thank them all personally.

Tuesday 13th December

After showering I did my exercises. It is great to be doing something at last albeit in small doses. Afterwards I would lay back on bed put my Christmas music on and longingly gaze up to Cosham hill to watch with envy all the dog walkers enjoying the outdoors.

I snuck into the gym to try the exercise bike. Crikey I could hardly get my leg over the low bar to get on the damn thing. When I finally did it I could hardly move the pedals. Hmmm this was going to be harder than I thought. I managed all of 3 minutes. Ugh!

Dr J the Psychologist asked me into her office for a chat. I told her that I would heal quicker if I could get home. To be with Bob, sleep in my own bed, be surrounded by my own things, get some fresh air whenever I wanted. I was willing to go home with the NG tube as I was now doing it all myself anyway. She was a very good listener and I poured it all out, my fears and my frustrations. She then told me that the team had been discussing the possibility of me going home. My eyes lit up `When ` I asked. My heart leapt when she said within the next week.

So the next few days were very busy.

The specialist nurse came to talk about the NG for home use and also the possibility of a `PEG` God I hope not. The thought of being fed through a tube that stuck out of my stomach didn't thrill me at all! The thought really scared me, will I have to be fed this way for ever or will I eventually get my swallow back?

Fungus worked on getting me stronger, giving me more and more exercises to do.

Dr B came to check my drugs and was horrified at the discovery that some idiot from Southampton just before my transfer here had written down the wrong dosage for my steroids. I was being given 2.5g Prednisolone instead of 75g. `No wonder you've not been feeling too good since you got here` she lamented. She was angry and I thought I wouldn't like to be that doctor who had written up my notes. Although I was just glad that she had come today and sorted it out. She also doubled the dose of Pirastigamine to see if she could boost up my energies.

Wednesday 14th December

Not much sleep as I`d had to have the extra steroid late last night and it had me bouncing off the walls till 3am. Steroids give you a huge adrenalin boost which kicks off your fight and flight responses. Your mind goes into hyper mode too. Steroids also increase your appetite. So many people put on weight when they're on them. However years ago, when I had taken them for my lupus I had read that the steroid cuts off the message from the brain that says `I`m full` so you still feel hungry. I had learnt to ignore that message and have a drink of water or a carrot or apple instead and I never did put on weight during the 6 years that I took the steroids. Be strong and ignore the false messages.

Fungus wanted to try me on some stairs as he knew that I had 13 of them at home, he wanted to make sure I would be able to manage. I did 24 steps. I took one step up two down. It took ages and I was so sweaty afterwards it was such an effort but Fungus was happy as he said we can `tick that box, safe on stairs` Yippee another hurdle. I could almost hear Buzz Armstrong`s voice` One giant step for mankind` I was grinning from ear to ear as Fungus patted me on the back and said `Well done`.

I was allowed now to venture outside on my own. Now you're talking. Whoopee! As long as I signed out in the book at the nurses desk and I kept to hospital grounds. Well they didn't have to tell me twice. I was off out to the car park to sit on the wall and look over Portsmouth to the sea. It was a beautiful fresh but sunny day and I sat there with my face up towards the sun feeling ecstatic.

On my way back in I bumped into Dr W who gave me a big hug and said he was so pleased to see me up and about . He wanted to know when Bob would next be in to see me as he wanted to meet him. I couldn't talk much as being out in the fresh air had caused my mouth to fill up with saliva again and my tongue felt too big for my mouth which was affecting my speech. If the doc hadn't known me better he would've thought I'd snuck out to the pub.

S.a.l.t came to assess my swallow. Tried a fruit puree with ice cubes in it. It made it easier to get down but it was still a very slow process. She also discussed the possibility of a PEG.

The specialist nurse brought me a present. It was a rucksack. Not just an ordinary rucksack. This was a specially designed one to carry my feed. This would mean that I could go out for walks and not be tied to Fred in the house. I had been wondering how I was going to push the great tripod around and the stairs had been giving me cause for concern too. All these worries were soon put to the back of my mind when I saw the little stand that I was to take home. It sat about 18inches high and it had a rechargeable battery which I could lift off and use in my back pack. It is clever stuff.

That rucksack was to prove an absolute godsend in the following weeks upon my release. The nurse showed me how it all worked and explained that all the supplies would be delivered to my home each month. All free too. Once again I thanked god for the NHS. I was also told how important it was that after I stopped the feed I had to flush the tube with water as the feed was very sticky and the tube could easily get blocked. If that happened it would mean another tube having to be put in. I could also vary the speed of the feed now that I was used to it, I could put it on when it suited me. Some people put it on at night and sleep with it on. I didn't fancy that as it meant you had to sleep sitting up.

Doctor came to say that I no longer needed the stomach injections as I was now much more active. Yippee! Another hill conquered.

Thurs 15th December

I slept well. Arms still feel very weak though my legs feel stronger. Tried to use the hairdryer but couldn't get my arms up high enough. I was desperate to try to improve on the scarecrow look as my friend Anita had called me yesterday, charming.

Later that day however I was able to lift my right arm up through my body to hold it above my head. I looked like I was about to ask the teacher `Please miss I need the loo` It was another hill climbed.

I had just finished ½ hour exercise routine and some stretches when Fungus found me in the gym `I always know where to find you` he says. He wanted to show me the Wii-fit. We spent the next ½ hour playing it's a knockout.

After all this exertion I felt exhausted and went for a lie down.

Doctor B came to tell me that the PCT had approved my 3, 4- Dap. That was indeed fabulous news. Apparently it had caused quite a stir as the head pharmacist had never heard of it and she had worked there for years. That shows you how rare LEMS is. As there was only one company who make it the drug was being couriered down from somewhere up north. I visualised a squad of cop cars whizzing down the M1 with the sirens going and a voice shouting out Special delivery for Deborah Pentland.

Dietician has now put my calories up to 1875kc a day. I`m on a `pig out`

Dr B met my Bob today. Just as she was leaving Dr W came in as he had promised to meet Bob and to see how I was getting on. He stayed for a long chat. He told Bob that he had come to know me over the years and he knew that I would come through this with my positive attitude.

I also mentioned to him that as there was no information for patients available on LEMS I was thinking of putting together a leaflet for patients. I thought it would be a good idea to include photographs of the before and after of the muscle loss and gain. He thought that a great idea and said he would arrange for a medical photographer to take some pictures. I really felt that if patients in the future could be given some information it would show them that it is not all doom and gloom.

Friday 16th December

I didn't sleep very well. It's the steroids. Now that the dose is back up I am awake until 3am. My mind is so active. The big worry is what the results of the PET scan will be. Will I have cancer?

I did my Harry Potter, then the gym for a ¾ hour session of exercise and stretches. I was just on my way back to bed for a rest when Fungus walks in to take me for some Wii-fit exercise. He wanted to get me on some new games to improve my strength and balance.

Just as he was setting it all up in walked Julia, Anita and my yoga friend Linda. So Fungus set us all up for a challenge.

What a laugh. I laughed so much my sides ached. To see my friends bouncing up and down, dodging the big ball in it's a knockout was hilarious. We played several different games and by the end of it we were all in hysterics, worn out and ready for a cup of tea.

The Games/TV room is the patients and visitors lounge. There are tea/coffee facilities where you help yourselves. It is also the only room on the ward to have any Christmas Decorations. A big tree sits in the corner and the room looks very festive.

The girls put the kettle on for tea and in walked Bob and Gary. They both wondered what all the noise and laughter was all about. I told them that my friends had just been letting out the inner child and making a complete ass of themselves. We all laughed together. As for Fungus I think he thought we were all nuts.

They all sat swigging their tea and enjoying their biscuits while I sat with the usual bag of sludge going up my nose.

Saturday 17th December

It was a beautiful morning outside. God I hope they let me go home soon. There's still no word.

I hope this weather holds for tomorrow`s marathon.

I did 45 minutes exercise routine and 3 minutes on the bike. I find I am now able to stand from sitting without using my hands today. I guess I must be a little stronger. Yippee! Another hill climbed. I walked out to the car park. The cool fresh air on my face felt wonderful. I sat enjoying the fresh air for about ½ hour.

On returning to the ward I saw that a Barber shop choir were just about to begin a Christmas concert in the foyer. I sat down to listen. The singing went on for about 45 minutes and I was glad that I still had my sunglasses on as there were tears streaming down my face. I was thinking that Bob and I should be listening together. Would I get home for Christmas?

After the concert was over I felt disorientated. I could not remember which corridor and lift I had to use to get me back to my ward. The Q.A is a huge hospital and thankfully there are always volunteers around to offer help. I swallowed my pride and went to ask a kindly looking elderly gentleman if he could help me get back to Phoenix.

He took me by the hand and off we went. He chatted as we walked asking me what I was in for, how long I'd been in and when did I expect to go home. I felt like an old biddy with dementia in an old fogies' home. I just felt so helpless. Eventually he got me to the correct lift that would take me right to Phoenix. We wished each other a Merry Christmas and said goodbye.

When I got back to my bed I felt emotionally and physically drained. I was also very thirsty. I actually managed to sip through a straw a whole glass of chilled apple juice. It tasted wonderful.

Sunday 18th December

I was awoken at 5.15am for my nose bag to go on. I then went back to sleep until 7am.when I did my exercise routine and then packed a few things for my big day out. This was it, marathon day.

Anita thankfully had managed to persuade the doctors to let me out for a few hours to see Bob and Julia finish their run. Julia's big day. I was so excited, but at the same time terrified.

For the last 6 weeks I had been confined to a hospital ward and I almost felt institutionalized.

Anita came to collect me, she too was very excited. Our friend Julia would join that elite group of Nutters oops I mean runners who had completed 100 marathons. I would have hated to have missed this. Bob had written to the organisers of the race and asked if they could possibly make sure that Julia be given the race number 100. They had obliged. So she would be wearing that number today.

It was a bitterly cold day but the sun was shining and the sky was blue. I struggled to climb into Anita's car. I saw that she had her bike in the back. She was going to cycle back along the route to cheer them on during the last few miles along Southsea seafront. There was also a bottle of champagne and a balloon with 100 emblazoned across it in the back with her bike.

We parked up by Canoe Lake. This was normally a very quick walk for me to the Pyramids where the race was to start. However it didn't take me long to realise that it was going to take me a lot longer than usual today.

I had my back pack feed on and I was parcelled up. With the bitterly cold wind in our faces I felt like Scott of the Antarctic. I found breathing difficult and my mouth was filling with saliva again. I felt like the NG tube was going to choke me. Oh please let me be ok.

We finally made it to the HQ. Julia's husband Mick was there all set up with a table decorated for a party. There was the huge chocolate cake, Champagne and glasses, balloons and a big 'congratulations' banner. Mick went to get a sleeping bag from his camper van for me to snuggle into. I've got thoughtful friends.

I sat there on a bench on the promenade in my sleeping bag looking like a homeless person. A lot of my running friends were there and they were all fussing around me making sure I was warm enough.

It was a glorious day. The sky was blue with hardly a cloud to be seen. The sea was whipping up the waves that were crashing onto the beach. It felt wonderful to be here. I usually spent a lot of time on the seafront and I had really missed it.

Before long I could see Bob come into view. With only a few yards to go I could see he was working hard but he looked strong. I wanted to jump up and throw my arms in the air and shout. I couldn't do any of that, so I just sat there smiling and felt the joy inside. My heart was filled with pride as he crossed the finish line and I saw him be presented with his medal.

Bob came over to give me a big hug and a sweaty kiss. All the emotion was making it hard for me to breathe so I had to really concentrate on trying to breathe deeply. Everyone was trying to talk to me and I couldn't answer them as my facial muscles weren't moving very well and I had a mouth full of foamy saliva.

Bob went for a shower and I watched as more and more runners came over the finish line. I wished I could be one of them. I realised at that moment how much work I was going to have to do to get myself back to that kind of fitness. It was a daunting prospect, but seeing the look on all those victorious faces was a great motivator. I would run again. It might take me a while but I would do it.

I had time before Julia was due in to go to the loo. I climbed out of my sleeping bag. It was freezing! I started to tentatively climb up the ramp; I wasn't going to even attempt those stairs. As I got to the top I could hear the alarm going off in my back pack. Oh no, that meant that there was a blockage in the tube, I would have to sort it. I crouched down, took off the pack and sorted it out. I went to stand up. I couldn't do it. There I was plonked down on the ground in a heap. I probably looked like I'd just done the run. Oh God what do I do now? So I swallowed my pride and asked a couple of young runners to help me up. Thankfully when you have a tube up your nose people realise that you're not well, they looked at me sympathetically and they happily obliged.

When I went into the warm conference hall it was crammed with tired and exhausted runners either refuelling or rubbing deep heat into their sore muscles. The aroma was overpowering but so familiar. I joked with some of my friends that what they need is a nose bag like mine to replenish their electrolytes. I won't repeat their replies. Suffice to say they weren't keen on the idea.

Back out at the Finish line Julia was coming into view. Anita ran alongside her to hand her a bottle of champers and her `100` balloon. As she approached the finish line she suddenly saw me. I must've looked like I'd just popped my head out of a tent at Everest base camp. The look on her face was priceless. `What are you doing here` she shouts with a huge smile. We all cheered as the commentator said those magic words. ` Congratulation to Julia this is her 100th marathon. `

I was now crying with emotion. I felt I was going to choke and started to panic. My airway felt blocked and I thought I was going to have to pull the tube out. Anita was quickly by my side and stroking my back encouraged me to breathe slowly and deeply. I did and my breathing returned to normal. It was a very frightening moment.

Meanwhile Julia was making her way over to us and we all went over to the party table for the president of the 100 marathon club to present her with her well-earned vest and medallion. Three cheers went up and the champagne corks were popping. The cake was cut and everyone was tucking in to Julia`s chocolate cake. I looked on wondering if a slice would go up my tube. Julia promised to put a big piece in the freezer for me until I could eat again. Mick joked about putting some champers up my tube and sending me back to the hospital drunk as a skunk. I don't think the Sister would have approved.

Once all the celebrations were over it was time to leave them all and head back to hospital. By now I was very cold, my hands were numb and I was exhausted but it had been worth it. What a super day.

When Anita got me back on the ward I got straight into bed and drifted off to sleep but not before giving her a big hug and thanking her with all my heart for giving me this wonderful day out.

Monday 19th December

I had slept well but I felt emotionally drained and exhausted after the excitement of my outing yesterday. However it had been well worth it.

It was a dark and gloomy morning as I looked out over Cosham hill. Wet and windy, but how I would love to be out in it. I managed a cold fruit puree for breakfast then managed a shower;

however the scarecrow look was still on for today as I couldn't manage to lift the hairdryer whichever way I tried to do it.

I went into the gym to do my exercise routine, and when I was on my way back to the ward the doctor appeared with a big smile on her face to say those words I'd been longing to hear. `You can go home tomorrow, we`ve all agreed that you can cope very well at home` I could've hugged her, if I could've got my arms up high enough. I wanted to jump up in the air and do a double backward somersault but hey I`ve never been able to do that anyway.

I had climbed this mountain on all fours but I had finally made it to the top. The view was grand indeed.

Fungus asked me if I had any concerns about going home after 6 long weeks in hospital. `How long have you got` I replied?` No seriously, the one concern I have is how I will manage my bath, I don't have a shower` So, Fungus practical as always took me into the gym and I had a few goes at getting up and down from the floor. This was the stuff I usually teach in my falls prevention classes and I found it quite humbling to be on the other side for a change. Once again I thought how important these functional exercises are. They help people to be able to do those simple tasks that most of us take for granted which in effect allow them to stay independent and stay on in their own homes. Not for the first time I felt a real joy in my heart at knowing that I played a small part in that. I just hoped that I was going to be able to get back to teaching.

It was a very busy day today. Word was on the streets. I was going home. They all wanted to come and say goodbye and wish me well.

Fungus gave me a huge hug and said that he would keep `tabs` on me through his colleagues in outpatient physiotherapy to see how I was getting on. Dr J the psychologist gave me a high five, Sophie the s.a.l.t came to check I had everything I needed for my NG, the other physiotherapists told me that they wished all their patients would commit to their exercise as I had done, the dietician and all the nurses came to wish me well and told me to let them know how I got on.

Later on Dr B and Dr W came to see me off and said they would both be seeing me in outpatients. In amongst all this kafuffle the Medical Photographer arrived to take me down for my `photo shoot` I felt like Twiggy. Mind you these days I looked like Twiggy.

The Photographer was ever such a nice chap, very sensitive. We chatted as we walked along the corridor to his studio.

Once inside a female assistant appeared to help me get undressed and she explained the procedure to me. I was allowed to keep my undies on if I wanted to however I wanted these photos to show the full extent of my muscle loss and that could only be done if I was naked. Thank goodness I'd been able to shave my legs and under my arms.

It was like a professional model photo shoot although I was no Nell MacAndrew. The walls were pure white, there were huge white umbrellas and the whole room was lit brightly.

The photographer said I was very brave for going nude but also thought it would produce much more accurate pictures. Well the photos weren't for the Sun Newspaper were they? He did tell me that medical photos always had the heads taken off, so anonymity would prevail. As I hoped these photos would go into an information leaflet for LEMS I was glad to hear it.

The photo shoot took about ½ hour. I was photographed from front, back and side views. I could see myself in the big mirror on my right. It wasn't a pretty sight. My once well-toned gluteus (bum) was now a saggy bag of flesh, my runners quads (thighs) had completely disappeared. My arms although never quite Kelly Holmes like now looked skeletal. I looked like someone just released from Belson. The only bit of my body I still recognised were my boobs, thankfully they had somehow survived the onslaught.

I would be very keen to see the photos for myself when I had my next appointment with the docs. I was hoping to have another shoot in a few months' time when I had built up my muscle mass again. It would be very interesting to see the comparison of the `before and after`.

After the session was over I got dressed and walked back to the ward smiling. I felt like dancing, I wanted to jump up in the air and click my heels together. Home tomorrow, Yipp a dee doo da! I hummed quietly to myself.

Tuesday 20th December.

`Escape from Alcatraz`

Anita had insisted that she would take me home. It was her day off, but she said that she did not mind driving into town to come and pick me up, that's what friends are for she told me.

The specialist nurse brought me a month's supply of feed and supplies for my backpack. She discussed again the possibility of me needing to get a stomach peg if my swallow didn't return as the NG tube was not a long term option. It was prone to infection if used for too long so usually if the condition persisted then a tube was inserted into the stomach and I would be fed through the peg. The very thought of being left with a permanent tube sticking out of my stomach sent shivers down my spine.

The last thing to sort out was my drugs. I would be given a 2 month supply to see me through the Christmas Holidays. They had managed to get me the 3, 4- Dap. Phew, Thank God! Dr P smiled at me and said ` You were a bit of a conundrum, but I'm glad that we were able to sort you out in the end. I was grinning from ear to ear as I said `So am I doc. `

It was turning into a bit of a party around my bed and I felt wonderful. All these wonderful people who had played a hand in getting me well. I was getting quite emotional as each one hugged me warmly. It was exactly 6 weeks today I had been in hospital. It felt like 6 months. Oh Boy! Am I ready to go home?

Anita`s smiling face appeared around the ward door, she was pushing a wheelchair in front of her. My face must`ve dropped at the sight of it. Is this who I am now? An invalid. `I don't need that ` I said. `It's not for you. If you think we`re carrying that lot you're insane` I laughed.   Looking at what I had to take home ` I think we`ll need a truck` I joked, we piled all my stuff onto the wheelchair, Anita could barely see over the top of it. Clothes, books, get well cards, feed, syringes and drugs. We were ready to go.

Everyone gathered together for a group photograph. I was trying to hold back the tears but to no avail. I was going home. I had thought not so long ago that I would never get out of here alive and here I was walking out and I felt as if I was walking on air. `Let`s go, before they change their mind` I joked, everyone laughed.

It was a struggle to get into the car but Anita helped me in and she had to do up my seatbelt as my arms and hands weren't strong enough.

On the 25 minute drive to my home I felt as if I'd been away for months. A new block of flats had popped up where a pub used to be. The trees were now all completely bare, whereas the leaves had not even begun to turn their autumnal colours before I had gone into hospital. It was a cold damp day but everything looked wonderful.

As I unlocked my front door and stepped into my usually warm and welcoming house it felt cold and unloved. Instead of the usual fragrance of fresh flowers it smelt damp and unlived in. Walking into my lounge I could see a vase of dead dried up 6 week old flowers still in a vase, as I looked into the dining room, the same thing. I burst out laughing. I ask you what can you do with men. Bob hadn't noticed that the flowers had all died he had not noticed either that the smell from the vases was permeating the whole house. I then spotted my house plants they too had been neglected and they all looked as if they`d died of thirst.

I turned on the heating, lit a couple of fragranced candles and put the kettle on. I huddled onto the sofa with a hot water bottle while Anita enjoyed a hot cup of tea. How long was it since I had had a hot drink? I looked on longingly and joked with Anita that as soon as my swallow returned I was going to have a huge mug of steaming hot tea and a whole box of mince pies.

By now my wee house was coming back to life. One thing I did notice was how small everything seemed after the big open hospital but that just added to the feeling of cosiness that was now enveloping me.

Home! I couldn't stop smiling. I am home and it`s still 4 days until Christmas. I couldn't wait for Bob to get home from work.

Wednesday 21st December

I had slept 8 hours straight through. The first proper sleep I`d had in 6 weeks. How wonderful.

Neuro Gym phoned to say they had an appointment for me tomorrow. I declined. As I had just escaped I wanted a few days to acclimatize myself to being home. They understood and rebooked me in for December 28th.They would arrange transport to pick me up.

Next the dietician rang to make me an appointment at the clinic, s.a.l.t rang to do the same. Although I was out of hospital they were obviously still going to be keeping a close eye on me.

I was now managing to drink the vanilla Fort sips .(300kc a bottle) As long as I put ice cubes in the glass to make it really cold I was able to drink properly through my mouth. It felt wonderful, although Ice cold drinks in the depth of winter are not ideal, but hey I was just so pleased to be able to drink anything. What this meant was that my swallow, albeit slowly, was returning.

Bob got out our little 2´ Christmas tree which we normally put in out conservatory. This year though this would have to serve as our main tree. We usually got a big real tree which we would carry together up from our local shop. It looked tiny sat in our bay window, but Bob promised that next year we would get the best tree ever. I normally decorated the whole house for Christmas but this year all that mattered was that I was home and we would be together. As for Christmas presents the only present we wanted was for me to get home in time. So we were very happy. Hell I was happy to be alive. What else do I want for Christmas other than that?

 I had been keeping a diary in hospital I decided that I would keep it up until I felt that the old me was back. I thought it a good idea to take some measurements and to keep a chart of my progress. That way I would be able to track my improvements and even if they were slow having a chart would keep me motivated to keep up the workouts.

My measurements on release from Hospital

I was determined to follow Fungus`s exercise programme and do it daily without fail. I wanted desperately to get my fitness back and I was willing to work harder than I had ever worked before to achieve it.

Thursday 22nd December

 I slept well again. I walked up to my GP weekly blood tests. Then I strolled slowly had taken my shopping trolley with me. I neighbour`s walls a couple of times to rest

Hips	34"
Thighs	18"
Calf	13½"
Waist	26"
Bicep	10"

surgery to arrange my around to my local shop. I had to sit down on and when I got into the shop I had to swallow my pride and ask a young assistant to help by carrying my basket for me. Of course once again the sight of a tube stuffed up your nose is all it takes for someone to realise you`re not well. Not for the first time I thought `This is not my life`

As I walked slowly back home with my trolley thinking how horrendously hard it had been I still felt good. I had achieved my first goal since getting home. I had climbed that first hill on my road to recovery. I had managed my first walk and my first shop.

Dr B rang later that morning and said `I've got a Christmas present for you, Your P.E.T scan is All Clear` I could feel the tears welling up, but her next words froze them in their wake. `That `raisin` we found under your right arm is a reactive node, we don't think that its anything to worry about but we've arranged for a biopsy with a specialist in oncology just to be on the safe side.` They would be in touch. Oncology – Cancer Oh God! ` Snakes and Ladders`

Just after having a bath (another hill climbed) I realised that in my excitement I had forgotten to flush the tube out when unplugging myself. It was blocked. I tried to clear it with syringes of warm water but it was hopeless. The warm water was just splashing up and showering me with spray. I thought back to another time in the hospital when the NG had blocked. The nurse had tried to flush it through too with warm water only to be showered in a spray. What she suggested next filled me with horror. She told me that when they have had trouble before with these NG tubes they use coke to flush the tube and that usually clears the blockage. I told her I didn't doubt it but there was no way they were going to shove that junk into me. I also told her about the U.S Road Police and their use of the stuff. I found it hard to believe that this was the usual procedure. Oh No, here we go again I thought.

Bob was late home from work; Posties are particularly busy this time of year. He found me in tears. We would have to go up to the hospital to have another NG fitted.

We got into our old camper van. The battery was dead as a dodo. We took a taxi and arrived at my old ward to be welcomed by Emma. Thank goodness it was Em on duty; this wouldn't be so bad after all. Emma joked with us saying `You've been trying to stuff a mince pie up there haven't you` Her kind and warm personality instantly calmed me.

So it was that number 4 NG tube was inserted. Poor Bob looked horrified as he watched Em putting in my tube. He had not seen any of the others going in. Let's hope that this one will be my last.

Not flushing my tube out had been a costly mistake; apart from having to get another one put in it had cost us £20 in taxi fares.

Friday 23rd December.

I awoke at 3am with an extremely dry mouth. I swabbed it out with a soaked sponge on a stick and went back to sleep.

Once up I did my exercise routine and put on my nose bag with my ruck sack on so as I could move around the house more easily. I felt shattered and one look in the mirror told me I looked it too. Something was going to have to be done about my Scarecrow look. I phoned my hairdresser and explained the situation to them. Thankfully they'd had a cancellation and they could fit me in on New Year's Eve. How lucky was that?

Saturday 24th December

My first thought on awaking was to get out for my daily walk. I got my feed rucksack on and took off for the park just beyond the local shops.

It was a crisp frosty morning. The air was fresh and there was a real nip in the air. There was a dusting of white everywhere I looked. The birds were all singing. It was pure joy that filled my heart as I sat there on a park bench enjoying the scenery. I was acutely aware of everything around me. The shapes of the trees, the patterns the frost made on the path, the silver shimmer of the dew on the cobwebs. Everything looked to me like I was seeing it all for the first time. I knew there and then that my life would never be the same again. I would appreciate every day of my life that I was to have ahead of me.

As I sat there deep in my thoughts I heard that wonderful whistle that the starlings make and I turned my head to see a few of them splashing about in a puddle having their morning wash. I puckered my lips and low and behold a noise came forth. I had got my whistle back. I did it again. I must have looked a funny sight sitting there parcelled up like Ranulph Fiennes on an arctic expedition. I tried some more tongue exercises. Poked my tongue into either side of my mouth, stuck my tongue out, just as well there was no one else about. Hey I thought another hill climbed. Check it out!

When I got back from my expedition I had a steady stream of presents arrive. A poinsettia from June and Bill a couple from my Tai Chi, Eileen from my falls class popped in with a bottle of something bubbly. I`d better not put that up my tube. Gill one of my running buddies brought me a lily bulb. She told me that as I watched it blossom so too would my strength grow. Julie and Pete brought me a Christmas bouquet and some Christmas candles. A group of ladies from a church group I do exercise for turned up with a card and present from the whole group, everyone had signed the card and written in some lovely words. I thought how lucky I am to have such a lot of lovely friends.

Christmas Day

Bob and I always had an early morning walk on Christmas day and today would be no exception. I donned my back pack and off we went along the seafront. We managed to cover 3 miles although I did need to sit and rest a few times along the way, 3 miles. I was coming on leaps and bounds here.

What spurred me on were the words written on the side of one of the white beach huts in bold black letters.

A JOURNEY OF A THOUSAND MILES BEGINS
WITH ONE TINY STEP
Lao Tzu

We couldn't believe it. I thought, had someone put it there just for me? Bob thought it may have been put there for the marathon runners last week but whoever did it, THANKYOU. That inspirational quote would remain there for weeks until the council came to paint over it. It would make me smile every morning I walked past it. You see it had a special meaning for me. I usually ran 1,000 miles in a year. I had my photo taken in front of it and sent a copy to both Dr W and Dr B. They both loved it.

The only problem I had now that I was doing a lot more walking was that I was producing a lot more saliva and as I couldn't swallow it as normal, it was making me cough and I was getting that awful feeling of choking. I could also feel the tube in my throat wiggling about in the sea of foamy saliva and it felt very uncomfortable. I had to mop up the foam with hankies.

As well as my daily exercises, I was determined to eat healthily. I was juicing. For Christmas dinner I had a carrot, celery, and apple and kale juice. Bob had turkey and the trimmings. One consolation was this would be one Christmas I wouldn't put on any weight. Now there's a silver lining!

I also found today that I could get up from the floor. It wasn't easy, but do-able. Another hill climbed.

Boxing Day

I walked 3 miles again, plus added on another few yards. I slept for 3 hours in the afternoon and then more exercise before a nice bath.

27th December

I walked a bit further than yesterday and I didn't stop so much. I even managed to do some ironing which was a major achievement when you think a few weeks ago I'd never have been able to lift the iron. Yet another hill climbed.

28th December

I did a 4 mile walk this morning. Afterwards I waited for the promised transport for my physiotherapy session but it didn't show up, there had been a mix up at the hospital, so I just did my usual exercise routine at home.

29th December

I walked 3 miles today but there was a very strong wind which made it much harder. As I sat down on a bench to rest I spotted our resident grey seal just out in front of me. He popped up looked straight at me before diving back into the choppy waves. Walking back I looked up when I heard a huge flock of geese flying in overhead. It is a fabulous sight and a sure sign that winter has arrived.

When I got home I was very thirsty and I drank a glass of water straight from the tap (no ice) it went down without any trouble. Whoopee! The song `Ain't no stopping` us now` came into mind as I danced around the kitchen. I then had a big glass of freshly juiced carrot, celery, kale and apple. No ice. It was delicious.

30th December

I awoke with a very dry throat again. This was becoming a problem for me. I now kept a flask of cold water by my bedside so as I could take a drink whenever I woke up. It helped.

I walked down to our local shops. Andrew our greengrocer asked me what had been happening to me as he couldn't help but notice my NG. On leaving the shop he handed me a hyacinth bulb in a pot and wished me a speedy recovery.

As I came out of the shop Julia was there waiting for me. She had cycled down from her home about an hour's journey to come and join me for my morning walk. We did 4 miles and stopped at the beach café en route for a rest and a frappe, which I sipped through a straw. It was delicious.

Later that day I had my first real food. It was a ½ of one of Bob`s fishcakes. I can't tell you how lovely that tasted. My taste buds had been reawakened from a long sleep.

31st December.

I walked to the hairdressers. It was about 2 ½ miles away. The scarecrow look had to go. As I sat there looking at my reflection in the mirror I did feel a little odd. Who was this stranger who was peering back at me. I was also a little concerned about my nose bling, as the end of the tube hung over my ear and I joked with my hairdresser to keep well clear with her scissors. Once it was coloured and cut I felt wonderful, like a new woman. I looked more like my old self or at least I would've done had it not been for that awful tube up my snout. Bob picked me up afterwards in our camper; I was a bit tired and ready for a rest.

Lots of hills climbed today.

- 1st cup warm tea
- 1st cup warm soup
- 1st hot food. Cauliflower/broccoli/gravy.
- 2 finger kit Kat. (Well I did deserve a wee treat)

I thought I was going to finish the year off on a high. Then a letter plopped onto my mat asking me to go for a smear test. My mind wondered back to a previous experience with an abnormal smear years ago.

In 1995 I had had a letter to inform me that my smear test had found some abnormal cells. I was booked in for laser treatment the following week. `Abnormal, you mean Cancer` I was terrified.

My appointment day arrived. Bob was at work so I was on my own. I was led into a theatre by a nurse and introduced to the surgeon who was going to perform the removal of the pre-cancerous cells. I was asked to strip from the waist down and get myself comfortable in the operating chair. It was like a big dentist's chair with the one big difference. There were stirrup straps either side to put your feet into. Omg I thought. The nurses laid a blanket over my legs for decency sake, they then took up position one on each side and held my hand stroking my arms to try to reassure me. They could see how traumatised I looked. The surgeon then came and sat in front of me. I know you`re picturing the scene and cringing, well you can guess how I felt.

I was not prepared for what happened next. The surgeon kept popping his head up over the blanket to ask me a question. It was like a Punch and Judy show. `So I hear you`re an exercise teacher` then `can you give me a few tips on how to get fit before you go `, Where do you teach etc. etc. He looked so funny I couldn't stop laughing. Then he'd pop up again to say `keep still as I don't want to zap out any healthy cells. ` I told him to stop making me laugh then. The nurses were having a good chuckle too. It did take the humiliation out of the whole experience though and before I knew it the *procedure was all done. He told me he'd been successful in getting all the abnormal cells but I would need to have*

regular check-ups. I told him that hopefully he wouldn't need to do any more 'curtain calls' They all laughed. My Puppet

Master had been as good as his word as I've had the 'all clear' ever since.

1st January 2012

This was it .Happy New Year. Let's hope so.

Bob and I had a lovely 4 mile walk this morning although our normal New Year's Day routine is a long run. We were both just grateful that I was alive. Every day was a bonus.

I managed a bowl of porridge and a ½ banana for breakfast.

After breakfast Bob rigged up my bike onto a 'turbo trainer' (it's a stand you put your back wheel into so you can cycle static without having to worry about balance) which was something that I was working on. This would help me build up my strength and stamina. Disappointingly I could only manage a few minutes. It was so hard, when I think of the cycling that I usually did. I always cycled to all my classes and covered quite a few miles each week. This was going to be a challenge I could see but it wasn't going to beat me.

Monday 2nd January

I didn't get much sleep last night. These steroids have me bouncing off the walls. They increase your body's adrenaline release so you're 'fight or flight' response is on full alert. You feel hyper in mind and body. Great if I was about to start a Race but not good if you want to sleep and get some rest.

I walked 4 ½ miles today. I stopped at the beach café and had a cappuccino which I sipped through a straw just to be on the safe side. I didn't want to choke.

I did my exercises and a few minutes on my 'turbo' bike then I had a lovely bath and hey! I was able to use my hairdryer for the first time. My arms were definitely getting better. I also managed to walk up the stairs without holding on. Another hill climbed.

Tuesday 3rd January

It was a wild, wet and windy day. Did my 3 mile walk, didn't see a soul, no one else wanted to be out in this weather. I got thoroughly drenched and I loved it. When I got home I felt exhilarated. It just felt so good to be out in the world alive and kicking.

I managed to take my medications by mouth today. What a milestone. At last I thought I'm beginning to believe that I will get this tube out after all. I can't wait for that day. I even sucked on a triangle of Toblerone today. Now that definitely wouldn't have gone up the tube.

Wednesday 4rth January

This was my Physiotherapy induction day. I was really looking forward to getting started on my new fitness plan. The hospital sent a car for me. My Physiotherapist would be Vicky.

Vicky told me that no one in her department knew anything about LEMS so this was new ground for us all. We were going to work on my core strength and stability. I would not be doing any cardiovascular work yet. The only thing they seem to know about LEMS is that exercise can make it worse. I closed my ears to that one. I knew that exercise would make me better and I would prove it. I had that glint in my eye again but kept quiet for now. Anita had warned them about me. When they were deciding how many weeks I would need Anita told them `Deb won` t need that long, she will do her exercises daily and she will push it` I think they must've wondered what they were taking on. This was to be just an assessment today but I wanted to get started. While I waited for my transport home I walked around the car park a few times.

On returning home I took a walk up to the library to look up LEMS for myself. I went armed with pen and paper to take notes. This was before I got myself a laptop. Sitting there scrolling through the information on LEMS I now knew why no one at the hospital had wanted me to read about it. It was scary stuff. It appeared to look like everyone who contracted LEMS was going to end up with cancer. Everything I read was saying that I would get cancer within the next 2, or 3 years. It was very grim reading. There was absolutely nothing about the small percentage of people who are auto-immune and get LEMS as another auto immune disease on top of one they already have. I knew that I had to work on getting some information out there for others like me.

Thursday 5th January

I walked 4 miles this morning stopping off at my GP surgery to have my weekly blood test. There was no getting away from all these needles.

In the afternoon I felt so good that I went out and walked another 4 miles.

`A Willing Mind makes a light foot`.

Eight miles today. I can`t believe it!

Friday 6th January

I had an appointment with the dietician next week but I wasn't prepared to spend a moment longer than I had to with horrible tube stuck up my nose. It had been 2 months now and I couldn`t wait to get the bugger out. I telephoned to see if I could get an earlier appointment. They couldn't fit me in any sooner so I explained that I was now getting enough calories in by mouth and could I take it out myself. The Dietician was very understanding and her words were `Well if it accidently comes out while you`re sneezing, so be it, but you didn't hear that from me` Well, that's all I needed to hear.

I knew that when I could take my drugs by mouth without having to crush them first that it would be time to remove the NG. I wasn't going to wait until I was told by the dietician that I could do so. I stood in front of the mirror sounded a drum roll and watched as I pulled out the tube. I did a wee dance then I rubbed the side of my nose and smiled at myself in the mirror. Thank God. It was out. Yippee!!!!!

I had been keeping a daily food diary and working out my calorie intake to make sure that I was getting enough nourishment. My day would begin with a breakfast smoothie .It consisted of the following:

- 1 glass water
- ½ glass almond milk
- ½ glass vanilla soya milk
- 1 teaspoon wheatgrass powder
- 1 teaspoon maca powder
- 1 teaspoon hemp powder
- 1 teaspoon spirulena
- 1 teaspoon lecuma powder
- 1 teaspoon organic mixed nut butter
- 1 teaspoon tahini paste
- 1 teaspoon flax powder
- 3 teaspoon chia seeds
- ½ banana
- ½ punnet blueberries
- Handful of fresh spinach leaves

This would make up a highly nutritious drink which would give me vitamins, minerals, omega fats, protein and carbohydrates. It was a complete meal in a glass. It was also very tasty and easily digestible.

Everything that I ate or drank was put on the chart. The calories were added up to make sure that I was getting enough calories for my needs. The following is a copy of a typical week`s food intake prior to the tube being removed. I still did not have my full facial movement so chewing was still laboured a little but I managed by sticking to fairly soft foods.

Mon	Tues.	Wed	Thur	Fri	Sat	Sun
Porridge ½ banana	Porridge pear	Porridge blackberries	Porridge pear	Porridge ½ banana	Porridge Pear	Porridge Blueberries
smoothie	2 finger kit Kat	smoothie	smoothie	smoothie	smoothie	Smoothie
Juicer drink	Soup Pumpkin seeds	Soup Pumpkin seeds	Juicer drink	2x rice cakes and cheese	Soup I egg boiled	Roast vegetable and gravy
Fort sip vanilla drink	Smoothie Crumpet and butter	Mince pie	Potato and chickpea Dahl	Juicer drink	Juicer drink	Fort sip vanilla drink

Bubble and squeak	Chickpea Dahl	Potato and spinach Dahl	Veg and bean couscous	Chickpea soup	Veg and bean curry	Noodles pesto tuna
Yogurt pear	Soya mousse	yogurt	Fort sip vanilla	Fort sip vanilla	Yogurt strawberries	Fort sip vanilla
2 finger kit Kat	Square dark chocolate	2 finger kit Kat	Square dark chocolate	Square dark chocolate	Square dark chocolate	Square dark chocolate
Lots of water	water	water	water	water	water	Water

Now that the NG was out I felt really great. I`m on my way back, I even look normal. Well as normal as I've ever looked. Now the serious job would begin on my road to recovery. I had no idea how long it would take me to get back to fitness but I was up for a `Pagger` what we Scots call a fight. Looking back to my early Lupus days I had done my first race in 1998 and from there had gone from strength to strength, so much so that I had managed as I mentioned earlier to go without drugs for 14 years. I knew that if I could get myself fit again I could sort this bloody LEMS out too. Now that the tube was out I could eat my own food and not have to rely on that muck in the bag. I knew that it was supposed to be very nutritional and all that but hey I don't think I wanted to know what was in it.

`When Fate shuts the door,
climb in through the window`

I am going to do whatever it takes to get my life back.

- Do the exercises routine the physiotherapist`s give me daily
- Eat healthily
- Get plenty sleep
- Surround myself with positive people (which describes most of my friends)
- Hug anyone I can
- Walk daily going a bit further each day getting plenty of fresh air
- Cycle on the days I don`t walk

I watched the film `Chariots of Fire ` today. I just love that film. What an inspirational True story. I just love that opening scene with them all running along the beach to Vangelis music. It`s just what

I need to get me going. As Eric Liddell says when asked what makes him run so fast. `Where does the power come from to see the race to its end? It comes from within` Well that is where I must look to find my power. I will find it within!

I walked 5 miles today. The next few days were to bring a list of achievements:

- January 8th I walked 6 miles today without resting in between.
- 9th. I was signed off the dietician. However it wasn`t straight forward.  To my utter amazement the dietician was telling me that she wants me to eat all the things she knows I don`t normally eat. Full Fat milk, butter, cream, cheese, biscuits, cakes and pastries. I thought` she is winding me up here` but she wasn`t. She was actually serious. I could not believe what I was hearing. I told her there was no way I was going to eat all that stuff. She told me that she wanted me to put the weight back on. I told her that the weight I had lost was mainly muscle and that it would take time to put that back on. I also said that if I ate all the things she was telling me to that I would end up with clogged arteries and probably have a heart attack. She then told me that I needed fats in my diet. I told her yes but healthy fats. Avocado`s, tahini, seeds and nuts. I showed her my food plan chart. She said it looked very healthy.  I then asked her why don`t you give these healthy options to your patients instead of telling them to eat all that junk. Her reply staggered me. She said that if she gave her patients the list of foods I was having that they would not know what most of them were. I said `Well unless you inform them they won`t`. Unbelievable! No wonder we have a nation of fat people? I honestly felt like slapping her! Thank Goodness I wouldn`t be paying her another visit.
- A few weeks later I was talking to a friend of mine who was going through chemo for cancer. He told me that he had been given the same list of foods to eat and he was having a Danish pastry every day to try to put some weight back on! As you can imagine I did mention to him that there are healthier options. He was amazed that the dietician had not given him healthy alternatives. It cannot be right can it that the NHS is telling patients to eat all that stuff?
- 10th physiotherapy session. The transport drops me off ½ an hour early, so I walked around the hospital grounds until my appointment time. Time management is crucial in coping with auto immune disease. I only have so many hours of energy to spend so I have learned over the years to spend it very wisely.
- 11th My 1st bike ride. I managed 3 miles. It felt so good to be back on my bike, however I must have looked like a loony pedalling along and grinning from ear to ear.
- 12th 6 mile walk. I am finding it a little easier now.
- 13th Signed off s.a.l.t. My speech is almost back to normal and I don`t feel like a drunkard any more slurring my words.
- 16th Man came from the feed company to pick up my backpack and surplus feed bags and syringes. I was so pleased to see the back of that lot I hugged the guy and told him to thank all the team at `Frejuis` for such a wonderful service and especially the backpack which had been a godsend in my recovery. He said he wished all his customers would treat him to a hug. It had made his day.
- 17th The transport for physiotherapy didn't show up so I decided to cycle up to the hospital. It was 6 miles there and of course it would be 6 back but I put my heart rate monitor on

and left with plenty of time so I could take it slowly. I was concerned about over taxing my heart as Vicki had been emphasizing that I should not do cardio stuff in the gym.

- 18th I upped my repetitions of my daily exercises from 10 to 20. I felt a lot stronger now and my breathing was much improved.
- 19th Added in some sit-ups
- 20th After my 6 mile walk checked my pulse rate. It was coming down it was now at 58 beats per minute. I was getting fitter. My pulse rate in hospital had been up as high as 80.
- 21st After a 5 mile cycle I spent the rest of the day decorating my kitchen.
- 22nd After a 6 mile walk I did another coat of paint in my kitchen.
- 23rd Finished off decorating and tidying up the kitchen, it looked really good and I felt really pleased with myself. I find painting quite therapeutic. I then had a 5 mile walk along the seafront, it was a beautiful day.

24rth January

Today I was having my biopsy done by the Oncology Specialist to check out that `raisin` they were concerned about.

It was a wet and windy day so I had donned my water proofs for my bike ride. I got to the hospital for my early morning appointment, stripped off my soaking wet garments and sat in the waiting room longing for it all to be over. When I was called in the Oncologist explained to me that they were going to do a scan and a biopsy to check me out thoroughly. They were all very nice and made me feel very comfortable.

I had to strip off from the waist up and lie down on the plinth with my right arm up over my head. As I lay there I felt like Kate Winslet in Titanic having her portrait done by Leonardo D` Caprio. The worst part was the injection under my arm to numb the area. After the numbness set in it felt as if I was `being pulled and pushed but not painful at all. They did the scan and took 4 biopsies. Thankfully it didn't hurt much it was just a little uncomfortable. After it was all done I was told that there would be a big bruise and a little bleeding but nothing to worry about. I was told not to do anything strenuous for a while. I told them I had my physiotherapy session in an hours' time. As long as you don't do too much with your right arm you should be fine they told me.

They said they would try to get the results to Dr B in time for my appointment next week. My thoughts were that it would all be good news and that I would get the all clear once again. After all, the other scans had all been clear.

Afterwards I popped along to the `Friends` café for a cup of tea and especially to thank them all for the volunteer work they do. It was through these peoples generosity in giving up their time that funds had been available to purchase the portable DVD players on Phoenix ward. One of those DVD players had been my saving grace for my lonely nights during my rehab.

I ordered my tea and told the 3 ladies and 2 gentlemen who were running the café and shop my story. I told them that although they might not often hear how much they are appreciated they were all doing a wonderful job. I got quite emotional and I could feel the tears welling up as I could see that they were all quite touched to know what their volunteering meant to us patients. I gave them all a hug and by then we were all in tears. It was a very heart-warming experience for us all I think.

At my physiotherapy session today Vicky says to me `We`re going to let you start cycling now` that glint appeared in my eye as I said `Oh good, because I actually cycled up here today` she looked horrified and said `we`re going to limit you though to 10 miles a week` I smiled and said` Ah, well it was 6 miles here and 6 back` she then said well we`ll allow you 2 extra just this once. I didn't dare tell her that I had been cycling for well over a week now and I had covered a lot more than 10 miles. In fact so far I had clocked up 28 miles.

Wednesday 25th January

I`ve bought myself a laptop. As I am not allowed to work for a couple of months I thought it a perfect time to have some computer lessons. After all they are free and I have the free time. So I am cycling down to my very first class with my laptop in my ruck sack on my back.

The computer class is held in one of the community centres where I teach my Tai Chi classes and it was so nice to see all the staff again. They were very glad to see me but I think they were quite shocked at how thin I looked but they didn't mention it. They told me that all my class had been phoning in to ask for updates on how I was getting on and more importantly when I was coming back. They were all missing me and the Tai Chi.

I learnt how to e mail today. Now I could keep all my friends up to date with my progress.

Thursday 26th January

I have worked it out that if I take my steroids at night before I go to bed instead of the morning then I sleep better and I am not bouncing off the walls until 3am. This new routine was to work wonderfully from now on. I only took the steroids every other day so now they were working better for me. I was now back to getting my 8 hours sleep a night. I am sure that this was helping to speed up my recovery as the following few days I was seeing remarkable improvements in my overall health and fitness.

- 27th January I can now run up and down the stairs. Amazing!
- 28th I managed to eat a raw salad today. My chewing and swallow appeared normal now.
- 29th walked 6 miles with Julia today. Walked a bit quicker too, and I didn't feel sweaty with the effort as I had been feeling before. I must be getting fitter. Julia had also bought me my chunk of her marathon chocolate cake she had been saving for me.Yummy.

This week I have cycled 35 miles and walked 19. I have done my physiotherapy routine 6 days out of 7 as well. I thought it was a pretty good effort. I must admit I did feel very proud of myself.

Monday 30th January

I had a 6 mile walk and coffee at the beach café. It is so wonderful to be outdoors. I can`t tell you how good it feels after being cooped up in hospital for all those weeks. I felt on top of the world with only one cloud ruining my view. What was the biopsy and scan from oncology going to find?

A lovely old couple walking their dog stopped me on my walk to say how good it was to see me looking so well. I asked `Sorry, do I know you` to which they smiled and said `We`ve seen you out every morning walking along the seafront with your tube up your nose and the backpack on and we have felt really sorry for you but at the same time we`ve been admiring your commitment. Rain or shine you have been out. It is so nice to see that you no longer need the NG` I was quite touched. I told them a little bit of my story and they told me I was an inspiration. There really are some lovely people out there.

Tuesday 31st January

I can`t believe that I have been out of hospital for 6 weeks now. It has gone by so much quicker than the 6 weeks I spent in hospital. I had an appointment to see Dr B in outpatients this morning so after cycling up there I waited impatiently in the waiting room. When Dr B appeared to call me in I bounded up to her and gave her a big hug. Dr B told me that I had made her day as she was amazed at how well I was looking. The doc then tested my strength and again was very pleased with how far I had come on. The good news was that I could now start to reduce the drugs. I could start reducing the Mestinon to eventually come off them all together and I could start to reduce the steroids as well, hopefully with the intention of coming off those too altogether. I was very pleased with that.

More good news was to come. The results from my Breast Scan and biopsy were All Clear. After showing Dr B my exercise log I asked her if she thought I could run again. `I don`t see why not` was her reply and it was music to my ears.

I also showed the doc my muscle measurement chart and my food diary. She was very impressed and asked if she could have a copy.

Although I was doing a lot of weight bearing exercise and eating very healthily Dr B still thought it would be a good idea to have a Dexa Scan. As I was on quite a high dose of steroids she wanted to make sure that there wasn't any bone density loss going on. More tests, oh well actually it will be interesting to see what shows up although I would be surprised if there was a problem as I was doing all the right things to keep my bones strong.

Wednesday 1st February

I had a lovely morning, meeting friends for coffee and then having lunch with my yoga class friends. They were all so pleased to see me looking so well. Later I cycled off to computer class.

Thursday 2nd February

I went out early for my walk and was on the seafront just in time for the sunrise. It was a beautiful sight. I stood and watched as the huge orange ball snuck up over the horizon blazing a trail of warm orange light along the water towards me. It looked like a path laid out just for me. I felt a warm comforting glow emanate from it and I felt a surge of energy from within.

I broke out into a wee jog just from lamppost to lamppost then a recovery walk, and then jog again. It felt good to be running again albeit very tentatively.

Friday 3rd February

I wanted to see the sunrise again, so I got up early and took off. I was dressed in my running gear as my intention was to do the same as yesterday walk/run. However on seeing the sunrise along with the frosty morning it was so beautiful and once again feeling that surge of energy, I started to run. I couldn't stop myself. I just wanted to keep going. I was grinning from ear to ear and the fresh wind in my face just added to the euphoria. I must have looked a complete lunatic as I ran along the seafront laughing and screaming out Yippee, Yahoo!

Once I got back home I felt absolutely elated. I had just run for 1 ½ miles non-stop. Ok, it had taken me 40 minutes but that did not matter at all. After 3 months short of one day I was back. I decided that I had to get a photograph of myself for a keepsake so I knocked on Julie`s door. She took one look at me and screamed `You`ve been running` she then shouts up the stairs to Pete ` Deb`s been running` I hear Pete shout back `That girl is amazing`. Julie pulls me in to her house and gives me a big hug. We then step out into her garden for my photo.

Later that day I picked up my t shirt that I had ordered from the print shop. It was bright red (energy colour) with white letters on the front which read `I`M BACK` and on the back `FROM THE DEAD ` I felt as if  I had been snatched from heaven`s door and told by St Peter `Not Yet`. I got Bob to take a photo of me wearing that too. This was the t shirt I was going to wear when I got back to teaching my exercise classes. I knew it would make everyone laugh.

The weekend was spent walking and working out and I was now able to put my hand weights up to 3kg.

Monday 6th February

I went for a run again. This time I did 4 miles. It`s incredible. All that power walking that I had been doing daily has really paid off. I ran around Canoe Lake and up those steps. The very same steps that I had hardly been able to crawl up the day Anita took me down to watch the marathon. I ran back down them and promptly did them a second time laughing at myself as I bounded up. I felt like Sylvester Stallone in the Rocky film and I punched the air, I swear I could hear the theme tune too.

A lovely old chap walking his dog stopped to ask how I was. He too told me that he had been watching me out on my daily walks with my nose tube in and was very glad to see me back running. He told me that he had read an article in the local news a few years back on me and how I coped with Lupus through running and healthy lifestyle and had been wondering what had been happening to me.

Tuesday 7th February

I cycled to Physiotherapy for my session in the morning and in the evening we walked 3 miles into Southsea to meet Gary and Helen for dinner at the pub. It was Bob and my wedding anniversary and I was going to celebrate with a nice meal and a glass of wine, (just one). We had a lovely evening. Gary and Helen couldn't believe that I was the same person they had wheeled into hospital a few weeks ago.

The next few days I either walked or cycled at least 6 miles every morning.

Friday 10th February

I went back to work. Tai Chi. I was so excited to be back although I did wonder if anyone would turn up. After all it had been 3 ½ months since my last class. They might have found somewhere else in that time.

You can`t imagine my amazement when they all came through the door plus there were 4 new people too. I still had my class of around 50 people; I was very touched that they had not deserted me. I was hugged by everyone. I think the new people must have wondered what they had come in to as everyone was crying and saying that they were so pleased to have me back.

I got up on the stage to begin and I took off my sweatshirt to reveal the comeback t. shirt. Everyone started clapping and cheering and someone started up 3 cheers and hip hip hooray. I found it very hard to fight back the tears and I turned around to show them all the words on the back of the t shirt which got me another round of applause and then one of them started singing that old chestnut by Peters and Lee `Welcome Home, Welllllllcome` to my amazement they all joined in. I was struggling not to break down in tears and I just managed to get the words out and thanked them all for all the cards and presents that they had showered me with the last few months and we got started with our exercise. I was back.

I had not known before I had got ill how well thought of I was and I found it all very humbling. It felt so good to be surrounded by so much warmth and kindness. I felt energized by it all. I would never forget this time in my life.

When I got home I had the most gorgeous e card from Linda my yoga friend who had been in class this morning. The picture was lotus blossoms and Chinese lanterns which I still use now as my screen saver. The words `You are a True Inspiration` My cup was overflowing with the warmth of human kindness. What a wonderful day.

The following week I started up my falls prevention class for my older folks. I once again wore my t shirt and I got a similar reception from them too. Everybody hugged me as they came in the door. It was good to be back.

Monday 13th February

This morning I receive a phone call from Vicky my physiotherapist. `A little bird tells me that you`ve been running` (Anita) I laugh. `Yes, I was intending to do a walk/run around the block but once I started running I just felt so good I kept going. I only did 1 ½ miles` Vicky`s response was `It`s too soon, I`ll let you know when you can run again` I replied `I was fine there was no problems` I could tell by Vicky`s tone of voice that she wasn't happy with me. Her next words confirmed it. `Well if you won`t take my advice not to run, she paused, I don`t think you`re ready` I cheerily said `Don`t worry Vicky, I`ll see you on Wednesday` and the call ended. Oops!

I wasn't going to get into an argument over the phone. I knew my own body and only I knew when I was ready to run. I wasn't stupid I would take it gradually. Hey, I`ve not put in for a race... yet have I?

 The phone conversation confirmed to me that I made the right decision 3 weeks ago in not telling Vicky that I had been cycling for 2 weeks prior to her telling me she thought I was ready to start. Well she had been warned about me hadn`t she. Had she only known me she would have realised that I never stick to the rules. If I had then I would never have been able to manage my Lupus for all those years without medication.

`Do not follow where the path may lead,<br>Go instead where there is no path and leave a trail`

Dr B would later tell me at my regular check-up in November that she had received a letter from Vicky informing her that I was doing more than I was supposed to and that she was concerned for my heart. Dr B wrote back to re-assure her that there was nothing wrong with my heart, and that I did know what I was doing. I would not overdo it as my body would soon tell me if I was.

Friday 17th February

My Tai Chi class unbeknown to me last week had had a whip around and now presented me with £42 to treat myself to a present. I was told that on no account was it to go to one of my charity`s. I must promise to spend it on myself. Once again I had to hold back my tears as I told them I would take Bob out for a nice meal and thanked them all from the bottom of my heart. They all agreed that would be a good idea as I definitely needed fattening up.

That weekend I ran 4 miles on Saturday and 5 miles on Sunday.

Monday 20th February

I had just left my house to cycle to my first Monday Tai Chi Class in Southsea. Earlier I had had a lovely 3 mile run along the seafront and I felt raring to go. I had literally cycled as far as the top of my road to the roundabout when a stupid woman approaching and looking to her right forgot to look directly in front of her and she hit me square on. Boom, I was down and almost out. I couldn't believe it. I sat there on the hard cold ground and everything happened at once. A chap jumped out of his van shouting and swearing at the woman `How the f***** could you not see her she was right in front of you and she`s wearing a bright red jacket` he was ranting, a nurse on her way to work came to attend to me and told me my head was bleeding, she went to get some hankies to staunch the blood, a police car pulled up and 2 ambulances arrived , meanwhile another couple who happened to be neighbours of mine, were out for a walk ,came over to help. The woman who had knocked me over was in a worse state than I was. She was now out of the car and shaking like a leaf. She was ushered into one ambulance, me in to the other. I looked skywards and said `You`re having a laugh mate` I think the policeman and the ambulance guys thought I was concussed and confused as I then started to laugh. They asked me what was so funny I told them` It`s a long story`

Once in the ambulance I was asked to take off my jacket so they could take my blood pressure. You should have seen their faces when they saw what was written on my t. shirt. They burst out laughing. It was hilarious. Once again I said `It`s a long story`. Once more I thought `This is not my life` I thought `You can`t write this stuff`

I was taken up to hospital. As I had a head injury I had to be assessed. There I was once more being wheeled into hospital. I looked skywards again and said` I`ve a good sense of humour my friend but it`s rapidly running out`

I sat in A&E looking around at all the miserable faces. It wasn't too busy, only about 7 other people waiting to be seen. I heard my name being called out. As I walked towards the triage nurse he didn't even look at me. He grumpily says `follow me` once we are in the little room he still hasn't looked at me and is asking me what has happened as he looks at the computer screen. He takes my details and then tells me to wait outside and a doctor will see me as soon as he can.

Well I`m sorry but I couldn't let that go! I tapped him on his shoulder and said `Hey my friend, a smile wouldn't go a miss here. Don't you realise that everyone here is traumatised. They could really benefit from a warm, friendly smile and a reassuring manner. No one wants to see a miserable bugger when they`re worried sick about what is going to happen to them` He finally raised his eyes and looked at me and mumbled `sorry`. On walking back out to the waiting room all the other 7 people started clapping, they had all been listening. One of them shouts out `Good for you, someone needed to say something to the miserable bugger` Well that was it. I sat down and we all started chatting to one another. It really helped not only to pass the time but also to dampen down our fears.

In the meantime, two policemen had gone to Bob`s work to ask where to find him out on his delivery to tell him the news. Poor Bob. There he was going about his delivery when he hears the police shouting up the road `Mr Pentland, Mr Pentland` they catch him up and tell him `Your wife has been in an accident but she is ok. She has been taken by ambulance up to A&E. He thought `what now` thankfully the hospital is not far from where he was and he arrived just as I was going in to see the doctor. I was checked over and told I must rest for a few days in case there is any sign of concussion. `Enough is enough` I said as I looked skywards.

One of my friends said to me the next day `It`s the character that`s the most strongest that god gives the most challenges` I won`t repeat my reply.

A couple of days later I was to cycle to computer class .Luckily I had a spare bike as my poor crashed bike was a right off. I would have no trouble in the following few weeks getting the insurance cover from the idiot who had hit me as there had been several witnesses. I felt very anxious getting back on my bike, but I knew I had to do it soon. The accident had knocked my confidence more than I had expected. I felt very nervous as I journeyed to class but I got there in one piece.

Thursday 24th February

My check up with Dr W at Rheumatology went very well. The Doc was also amazed at how well I looked and he loved the t-shirt. I told him about my bike accident and he said `You don't do things by halves do you`

The following days saw me getting stronger and stronger. I was running quite well now and felt about ready for my first challenge.

Saturday 10th March

Each year Bob and I take part in a cross country run in Devon called the Grizzly. It is a 20ish mile race, run over the hilly Devon countryside, much of it on the coastal paths between Seaton and Branscombe. It is a very tough event. I knew that I would not manage 20 miles, however there is a smaller run called the cub which was only 9 miles, so I decided to do that one instead.

We always spend a week down there making a holiday of it. We set off on a lovely crisp fresh morning in `Hector` our old VW Camper. About half way there disaster strikes. Suddenly Bob felt the steering going, he couldn't control the beast and we were rearing off to the side. Thankfully he managed to get us onto the verge and I jumped out to see what was happening. Imagine our absolute horror when we saw that we had lost one of our back wheels. The thing had vanished. On searching for it we finally discovered it in the ditch a few yards from where we had landed. A lovely chap in a big van stopped to help and he and Bob got out the spare only to find it had a faulty valve and it wouldn't stay up so we rang the AA.

As we sat there in shock we both suddenly burst out laughing. Bob said ` Can you believe it` I looked up once again to the big fella in the sky and shouted ` I have a good sense of humour my friend but let's not over play your hand`

Eventually we got taken to a garage and sorted out with another wheel and we were once again on our way. Surely nothing else could go wrong from now on? Thankfully nothing did.

We turned up Sunday morning for the run. It was a beautiful sunny but cold morning. Luckily there are many people on cross country runs who walk a lot of it too so I was in good company. I was in 7th heaven. Being out in the great outdoors again doing what I love. I crossed that finish line with a beaming smile and both arms up in the air. Another hill climbed.

19th March

Another big step today was my return to the gym. (I had asked one of the Neuro-Surgeons to write a letter to my gym explaining my absence and asking if they could freeze my membership for a few months. They readily agreed. So I hadn`t lost out financially) I now felt that I was strong enough to go back to my 2 sessions a week if I took it gently to begin with. I found it hard. I had to bring the weights down from what I had been doing before but I knew that I would soon work back up again. I just had to be patient. What was funny was the first song I heard coming from the piped music system `what doesn't kill me makes me stronger` How appropriate is that then I thought as I pumped the iron. Later that day I popped into the t shirt shop and had those words printed on bright green t shirt.

Sunday 1st April

This was a very special day for me. It was my first real run back. I decided to run as a Jester (well it was April Fool's Day, what do you expect) This was the Bournemouth Bay Run where I was supposed to be running the Half Marathon but there happened to be a 10km on as well so I was going to do that instead, 13 miles would have been pushing it. Bob was running in the Half. My friends Gary and Helen would do the 10km with me and Gary was dressed in blue scrubs and had a stethoscope around his neck. I was going to send a photograph of this one to my doctors as I had promised to do on my first run back.

As this was just about the time that the Olympic torch was being relayed around the country I decided to make my own torch. I hadn't been lucky enough to be picked as a torch bearer but I could do my own torch run.

It was a fantastic run. It was another gloriously sunny day. The run takes place along the beach at Bournemouth with stunning views out across the bay. The final 2 miles of my 10km brought me running in the opposite direction to the half marathon runners just setting off on their first 2 miles. Every one of them on seeing me was giving me a cheery wave, a smile a high five or a clap. It really was as if they all knew what I had been through these past months. I felt wonderful. By the time I was crossing the finish line I was in tears. I had my arms up in the air and I floated across the line under the gantry to applause from the crowds. I had my picture taken with my medal and my t shirt and yes, a copy of it went to Dr B, Dr W and of course I just had to send a copy to Dr S on the ward in Southampton as I had promised I would.

Dr B has told me that Dr S has put it on the ward notice board for all to see.

Easter Weekend April 6th-9th

My next challenge was the 3 Hills on the Isle of Wight. Bob and I usually did two runs over the weekend but thought that I had better play safe and just stick to one event this year. The Easter Monday run is an 8 mile cross country run along the cliff paths over on the south side of the Island. Once again some stunning scenery was to be had.

Steve and Julie would be there too. This was a very special occasion as one of the photos that they had brought in to the hospital for me was us all at the finish line of this race last year. So it was going to be another emotional day.

The weather was foul, wet and windy and it was a struggle to keep your feet on the ground. Up on the top of Tennyson Down it was blowing a Hoolie, but none of that could dampen my spirit as I ran headlong into the wind I was shouting at the top of my voice Yahoo Yahoo. As usual I was right at the back of the pack and by the time most of the others were in the shower I was just coming into my last mile of the run. I was enjoying every moment though and before long I was running in towards the finish line and I was ecstatic. Bob, Julie, Steve and some others were all cheering and I once again crossed the finish line with an enormous grin and tears streaming down my face.

A nice hot shower and a big mug of tea soon put us all to rights and before catching the hovercraft home Bob and I went to the pub for a meal and a well-earned glass of wine.

Sunday 22nd April

Now I was ready for a 10 mile event. The Bluebell run in Worthing. How lovely to run through the bluebell woods in springtime. The only problem was Brian and I got lost, we somehow missed a marker and ended up doing only 9 miles instead. Not that I was worried as I was finding it hard, it was a very hilly run and tough going. The last ½ mile was up a very steep hill but we kept on going and made it to the finish smiling.

Sunday 6th May

This was to be my biggest challenge so far. It was a cross country half marathon and a very hilly one at that. What made this one particularly hard was that it was wet and windy and the terrain was like a bog. With my feet covered in sticky mud it made it very tough going. It felt like I was running with lead weights attached to my feet. Up on top the South Downs the rain was lashing so much that I could hardly see where I was going. The mist was also coming in and making it difficult to spot the arrows pointing the direction that we needed to go in. Luckily just as I was about to go off in the wrong direction another runner just behind me shouted to me and I was back on track.

 We ran together for the rest of the race, it is always nice to have someone to run with and chat along the way. I finally made it to the finish line and it had taken me about 3 hours. I was very pleased with myself .I had been running for 3 hours and I felt great. On crossing the finish line and being presented with my medal the winner of the full marathon was just coming in (they had started much earlier) He had done a similar time to me but had done twice the distance, but I wasn't deflated at all and we had our photo taken together, him with his `winners' cup` and me with my` tea in a cup` the only cup I was ever likely to get. It had been a fabulously invigorating day.

It felt good to get a half marathon under my belt as my big challenge that I was working towards was the Edinburgh half marathon which was to be at the end of the month the 27th May. Once again I was going to have to drop the distance. I had been entered in for the full marathon. ` Doctors orders` I was to come back gradually. So it was the half marathon for me this year.

I was going to run as a ragdoll for Myasthenia Gravis. My aim was to raise £1,000.

Bob and I had decided that we would have a week`s holiday staying with his parents in the centre of Edinburgh before the run. We had had a fabulous week catching up with both our families. We had also been so lucky with the weather. We seem to have had the warmest week of the year, it was glorious. Bob was suffering from a running injury and he would not be running so I was on my own come Sunday but I didn't mind. I was so looking forward to it and I was getting very excited.

Sunday 27th May

My big day had arrived. Thinking back to the hospital I didn't think I would ever have had a chance of getting fit enough to do this event, so I was on a high. What made it even better was that they forecast a sunny dry day.

After an early breakfast I donned my outfit. It consisted of striped black and red socks, red skirt, white flouncy blouse and red waistcoat, red tartan bow tie and my MG `Myasthenia Gravis` vest. Then topped it off with the blond wig which I had tied into bunches with red ribbons. Finally the finishing touches, a red tartan hat. I then rouged two big circles onto my cheeks and I was ready.

Bob walked with me through Edinburgh to the start line. It was a 3 mile walk but we were enjoying the nostalgia of seeing all of our old haunts again. We hadn't visited our home town for a few years and found it much changed. I was getting a few strange looks from people en route but they all smiled at me and wished me luck. Once at the start I still had about an hour to go so I kissed Bob goodbye and went off to find the loos. Bob was going to spend the day with his brother at the gym and I would see him later. I didn't want him to come to the finish line as there is nothing worse for a runner to watch a race that he knows he should be running in but cannot because of an injury. It is sheer torture, and I wasn't going to put Bob through that ordeal.

I had my camera with me so I was getting a few snap shots before the race began. One guy who was there to see his girlfriend off was wearing a bright orange sweatshirt with the words `I`m not a doctor, but I`ll take a look any way` printed on the front and a picture stethoscope hung around the neck. I had to get a photo taken with this chap. How appropriate is that? Next I found some other fancy dress runners so I got a few more snaps. By now it was time for the off so we all got into our time slot positions and awaited the start gun. They were playing music and the song `This could be the greatest day of your life `was blaring out to inspire us all.

The gun goes off and we are on our way. Well this is it I thought. Let`s hope I can keep running for the whole 13 miles. The route was fantastic. We went all around Arthurs Seat and the Scottish parliament buildings, making our way out of Edinburgh along the coastal road towards Musselburgh which is where the race was to finish. Before long we were running along the promenade on Portobello beach. This was very exciting as this is where I had learnt to swim years ago age 17 and I don't think I had been back since. It hadn't changed much. Thankfully it was still a beautiful little seaside village. As we all ran along the Prom there was music playing and the song was `What doesn't kill me makes me stronger` The same song I'd heard in the gym on my first visit back. How amazing is that.

As I ran along soaking up the atmosphere two other runners came along beside me and asked me what MG was. Also why was I running as a ragdoll? So as we jogged along together I told them a little of my story. They seemed very impressed as they knew someone with Lupus and knew how debilitating the disease could be, so for me to be running not only with Lupus but with LEMS as well they knew must be a real challenge. They wished me luck and off they went.

It was getting very warm by now and the sweat was beginning to pour down my face, the wig was slipping a bit but stayed on thankfully. The streets were lined with people cheering us on and the miles just slipped by until sooner than I had expected I found myself on the last stretch. I was almost there. I can`t believe it I had run non- stop for 12 miles I knew that I could keep going for just one more. Some chap shouted out `Go Dolly Parton`, I thought blimey my boobs are not that big, it must`ve been the blond hair.

As I rounded the bend the finish line was in sight and the crowds were very thick and very noisy. Everyone was screaming and cheering us all in towards that line and I could hear the tannoy playing the song `You`re simply amazing, just the way you are` Well that was it. The flood gates opened and I was blubbing like a baby. As I crossed the line under the gantry I threw my arms up in the air and let out a big holler Yahoo! I then punched the air. I had done it, 13 miles. And I had run all the way. I was over the moon. I was presented with my medal, t shirt and a goody bag and I went into the finish area to break down in tears of sheer joy and exultation.

 After I composed myself and was doing my stretches another runner came towards me. She looked very emotional too. Her next words brought the tears back to my eyes. She said ` I was running along behind you earlier when you were telling your story to those two girls and I just had to come and tell you that I think you are amazing`. Well I was very moved, so much so that I couldn't get any words out, I just smiled and the tears started to roll down my face. I hugged her and sobbed out `Thank you` We both stood there hugging one another and then she said `You kept me going. I was really struggling at that point and when I heard your story it spurred me on to the finish. Thank you`

We said our goodbyes and it was time to find the showers.

I walked into the ladies changing room which was filled with excited females all in various states of undress reliving various aspects of the race. When I walked in all heads turned. `F****** ell girl, you must`ve been sweating in that lot` cried out a Glaswegian lass. I replied `It was rather warm. Do you want to see a bad hair day` I then whipped off my wig and the whole place erupted in laughter. My hair was stuck to my head and my face was very red. I must`ve looked a sight. The next words confirmed it. `F***** Hell ` It was funny. You can always trust Glasgow lass to lift the mood a notch more.

They were still all talking excitably when I got into the shower. My God it was freezing but I wasn't going to spoil the fun for the rest by warning them. `Lovely shower` I said as I came out wrapped in my towel.

They all piled in the shower as I came out. I won`t repeat the expletives but suffice to say it wasn't `Crikey these are a wee bit chilly` what a laugh.

> `The most wasted of days is that
> On which one has not laughed`

Well this had definitely not been a wasted day!

After my cold shower I went to find the `Porridge `stall. It certainly beats a burger. I had a gorgeous bowl of hot scots porridge oats with toasted almonds and a chopped pear. It was absolutely gorgeous. By now the marathon runners were beginning to swarm in and I sat there on the kerb at the finishing straight enjoying the atmosphere. It was electric. A couple of hours later I was on the shuttle bus back to Edinburgh city centre where the race had begun. I had my medal and my t shirt on and felt tired but very satisfied. I had another 3 mile walk through Edinburgh back home to be met with a big hug and congratulations from Bob. We both said that we will have to come back next year and we would both do the marathon together. It had been a super day. In fact it had been a super week in Edinburgh.

During the summer I ran 3 times a week and did the gym 3 times a week. Saturday was my day off. I was getting much fitter and I felt a lot stronger. My 3 runs were all done early morning and I had turned them all into mini-triathlon`s. I would cycle down to the beach ½ mile away from home. I`d lock my bike up which had a towel, a change of clothes, a bottle of water and a piece of fruit tucked away in my panniers. I would run for about an hour, come back to do some stretches and then jump into the sea for a 10 minute swim. Afterwards I felt ready to take on the rest of the day. The sea water was very cold but very invigorating and it helped with all the aches and pains. I guess it just froze them out.

10th June

I was now able to stop taking the LEMS drug the 3, 4 -Dap. Great another one dropped and another hill climbed.

By now Bob and I were back to racing. Not every Sunday but we had at least one race every month.

- 24th June: North Devon Coastal half marathon. This is a beautiful coast path run, starting and finishing on Woolacoombe's 3 mile sandy beach. The scenery is stunning. It was a scorching hot day. I ran with my friend Julie, we had a super run chatting along the way and stopping to take photographs. Bob ran the marathon almost doing it in the same time we took for the half. He even won a cup for the first man over 50. I was very proud of him. Two years ago at the inaugural race, Bob had been looking forward to this run, but in May he had fallen during a training run on our holiday in Minehead, breaking his arm. He was determined not to miss out so he ran with his arm in plaster, and believe it or not won the cup for fastest man in his age group. He was rewarded with an enormous round of applause as he walked up to collect his well-earned prize. You see what I`m up against here folks. I am not the only one in the family who has that never give in approach. Another funny story is when the break occurred. We were lucky that Minehead had a small cottage hospital with A&E. We had been out running on Sunday morning when coming down through the woods Bob slipped on a muddy downhill bit it had been raining heavily the night before. We walked into A&E leaving muddy footprints everywhere. The doctor asked Bob to pop up onto the bed so she could examine his arm. At this point Bob came over a bit light headed, his blood sugar had dropped and he asked the doctor if he could have something to eat. The nurse disappears and returned quickly with a little cake to which Bob says `Haven`t you got anything healthier` The nurse looked surprised but went to get a banana which was part of her lunch. When she got back Bob had eaten the cake, but gratefully took the banana and wolfed that down too. The doctor and the nurse laughed. It was funny.

- 8th July: Chichester Challenge. This is a tough 16 ½ mile cross country run. The weather was changeable. One minute it was pouring with rain the next warm and sunny. Once again I ran with Julie. It was a tough run as everywhere was so wet. The thick mud was sticking to our shoes and making it very heavy going. However the stunning scenery made up for it. We had had so much rain in the previous weeks that the river had burst its banks and the last few miles we were wading through knee deep water on the normally dry path. It was fun though.
- 19th August: Isle of Wight half marathon. It was a scorching hot day and tough going. The run starts and finishes in Ryde. The hilly route takes us around the east side of the island taking in some stunning scenery. I had remembered from last year seeing a small shop at the top of a hill at the 10 mile mark and I popped in to purchase an ice lolly. So the next mile I was running with a huge smile on my face as I happily sucked on the ice cool orange pop. I felt a great sense of achievement as I crossed the finish line.

- 2nd September: The Stansted Slog is a half marathon run through the gorgeous Stansted country estate. It was a slog too. The weather was dreadful. Very wet, cold and misty. Yes I was the last runner in but hey I did it!

All of these runs were leading up to our favourite week of the whole year. Bob and I spent a week over on the Isle of Wight in Ventnor. We always took part in the South of England Fell Running Championships. It was a weekend of tough very hilly cross country running. On the Saturday there was a 3 mile run in the morning, an 8 mile run in the afternoon and a Half Marathon on the Sunday. This was the running event looking back where I felt my LEMS trouble must have all started.

Last year I had real trouble, particularly on the half marathon. My legs had felt so heavy, as if I was running through treacle. I kept saying to Lorraine (the sweeper) who was with me for most of the way as I was last as usual. 'I don't know what's wrong with me but I feel so tired' she knew about my Lupus and had told me every year at the beginning of these runs that she didn't mind how long I took, she would run with me. We had always enjoyed chatting as we jogged along. It was good to have company. I remember crossing the finish line on the Sunday, collapsing into a heap and bursting out in tears.

Well this year I was able to tell Lorraine why I had been struggling so much last year. She said 'Deb, you're just damn right greedy, not content with the Lupus and Raynaud's, you want another one' we laughed. Lorraine and I chatted during those three runs over the weekend. Towards the final few miles of the half on Sunday, just as we got to the top of the hill for the big panoramic decent back into Ventnor it became very windy and bitterly cold. I wished I had brought a jacket and gloves with me. However Lorraine had anticipated my needs bless her and produced out of her rucksack the very items. Like I said I have some very thoughtful and kind friends.

'When you get to the end of your rope.
Tie a knot and hang on'

We finally made it to the finish line and again I burst out in tears but this time they were tears of joy. We quickly got changed and went down into the hall for the Prize Giving Ceremony. Bob usually picked up a prize or two at this event and I wanted to be there to give him a cheer.

The organiser then came to the South of England fell running champions for the 50+ladies. You cannot imagine my shock on hearing my name being called out for the Silver medal. By heck I almost choked on my rice cake. You see although I had been last in all 3 races, you had to do all 3 to qualify for a medal. There had apparently only been 2 of us girls in that age group who had done all 3 races. How cool was that! I went up to collect my medal in tears and I gave the chap a big hug. I think he thought Blimey! Who is this nutter. All my friends were clapping and cheering. It was a fabulous moment for me. Wait until I tell the doc's about this! Oh and just for the record. Poor Bob didn't get a prize this year. Well to be fair he is 59 in the 50+ age category so he's up against it. Wait until next year when he reaches 60. Look out!

'Kites rise highest against the wind
Not with it'
Winston Churchill

This medal gave me the confidence for my next challenge. This would be my `Slaying of the Dragon`. The Beachy Head Marathon on the 27th October. That would be in just a few weeks' time.

Saturday 20th October

We arrive in Eastbourne. We`ve booked into a wee cosy cottage just at the foot of the South Downs. We`re having a week`s holiday before the race next Saturday.

It has been a very damp, misty week and I am worried about what the conditions will be for the run on Saturday. Bob and I had had a recognisance run on Thursday and we had got lost up there. The mist had been so thick you couldn't see your hand in front of your face. If we got this on Saturday it was going to be scary. It would only take one false step and you would be over the edge of the cliff never to be seen again. It was a massive drop.

During the week we had had a couple of training runs. We had also been out along the prom on our in-line skates and we had been to a yoga class for a good bit of stretch and relaxation. We were ready to go.

Saturday 27th October

My Big Day had arrived. This was what I had been working towards for the last year. As I sat enjoying my smoothie I couldn't help but reflect back to this time last year.

I recall just how I had felt on that morning and remembered only too well how I had struggled even to walk those first 9 miles. One of my friend`s Dad had picked me up in his car and was going to take me to the finish as I felt so exhausted. However as we drove on towards the Seven Sisters I began to feel a little better. So I asked him to drop me off at the Cuckmere River and I would walk the last 7 miles. Some friends of mine had promised to meet me there and run the final 6 miles with me so I would have company. They might have to carry me around I thought. My friends were there as promised and I struggled to keep up. We were walking most of it but it was The Seven Sisters, so very hilly. Finally they managed to drag me to the finish and I crossed the line. I slumped to the ground as I found my legs give way beneath me. Of course a few days later The LEMS really took hold and my ordeal began in earnest.

This year would be very different though I thought as I got myself ready.

We were both up at 05.30am. The forecast was good. It was going to be a bright day with the very slim chance of the odd shower. The only down side was it would also be bitterly cold with a very strong force 8 gale. So I made sure to wear plenty of layers, 2 pairs of gloves with hand warmers, waterproof jacket and my funny woolly hat. This hat always cheered everyone up and brought a smile to the faces of the marshals.

I felt really good and I couldn't wait to get going. I was going to start an hour earlier with the walkers as I knew that if I started with the mass start that by the time I got to the top of the first hill I would be left behind and spend the rest of the day on my own.

At 8am I set off. They had been right about the wind. Crikey, it hit me like a brick wall. It made the running really hard work but I struggled on. Before I knew it I was at Jevington which I knew was about 5 miles. The course then climbed up into the East Dean forest which was absolutely gorgeous. Autumnal colours made a beautiful carpet of leaves to run on as I ran through the woods. The birds were singing and by now I was out of the wind. I reached the first check point. It was around the 8 mile mark. I stopped for a quick cup of water and a piece of banana. I declined the biscuits and mars bars.

I ran on and it wasn't long before I reached the next check point at Alfriston. I had covered 10 miles. It was here that the lead runners began to fly past me. They didn't even stop for a drink. The lovely thing about cross country running is that they don't usually mark the miles. I don't really want to have to tick off each mile because I find it really plays on your mind. I just like to enjoy the scenery and keep going until I see the finish. As I`d done this run several times, I had a rough idea of how far I`d run. I had taken my camera around with me and I was getting some wonderful shots which Bob and I would enjoy looking at later.

Before I knew it I was at the 17 mile check point. I always remembered this one as they always served us hot tomato soup, tea and sausage rolls. There was also usually a trio of musicians playing here too. However disappointingly there was no music today. I sat down for a wee break and enjoyed a hot soup, savouring every warm mouth full. I declined the sausage roll. I then had two cups of tea and a couple of bites of my energy bar and I was ready for the off again. Only 9 miles left to go. Single figures I thought.

The next part of the run is up a long set of steep steps which go up through the woods. It looks very menacing from the bottom and proved to live up to its expectations. Phew! It was a tough haul. Usually there is a chap playing the Bagpipes at the top but no sign of him this year. I asked the marshal. `Where`s the piper this year` to which he cheerily replies. I`m sorry but you`re too slow, he`s gone home for lunch` Cheeky bugger I thought.

I carried on onwards and upwards towards the final and toughest part of the marathon, the 9 hills consisting of the Seven Sisters, Birling Gap and then the final hill, Beachy Head. Well I knew what went up must come down so although there were 9 up`s there was also 9 down`s.

Just as I was coming down the hill towards Birling Gap (22 miles) it started to cloud over and it got very dull. Suddenly the heavens opened up and it chucked it down. Oh oh! I thought, now we`re in trouble. We`ve still got an hour of running to do. What with the wind and the rain this was going to get really tough. I wasn't going to let it dampen my spirits though and I thought `If you want the rainbow, you got to put up with a bit of rain` Sure enough a rainbow appeared overhead and the clouds dispersed to reveal blue skies once more. It was stunning. I let gravity take over as I sped down into the check point where I gratefully accepted a steaming cup of tea and a piece of fruit cake. Yummy! Bob always wondered what took me so long on this run.

Feeling warmed and sustained I took off for the final 4 miles. I must admit it was definitely more walk than run at this point, but I wasn't alone. By now everyone was almost horizontal pushing onwards into the wind. It took all my strength not be blown backwards and I must confess to a few wee swear words coming out from my mouth. At least no one could hear me because of the wind.

Eventually though the finish line was in sight. The whole of Eastbourne lay before me as I came over the rise to start my descent. My speed picked up and my spirits were high. I had almost done it. I then saw Bob waiting anxiously for me. He waved and shouted `It`s all downhill now` I had to stop myself from crying as I needed to watch my step. If I had tears in my eyes it would blur my vision and one false step I would be getting to the finish line on my ass.

I reached the bottom of the hill safely and as I approached the gantry I heard the announcer calling out my name and number and I crossed the line with my arms above my head in a state of sheer euphoria.

I HAD DONE IT! I HAD` SLAYED MY DRAGON`

Bob ran over and threw his arms around me and we hugged enthusiastically. I was presented with my medal and I raised it to my lips and gave it a kiss. This was my 13th marathon. It was a very special one. I couldn't believe how quickly the year had gone. I broke down in tears. I had come a long way in the past 12 months. I had climbed several hills and conquered them all. I had been to hell and back. All those long weeks last year as I lay in that hospital bed I wasn't sure whether I would ever walk again let alone run. But I had worked hard and all my hard work had paid off. I had come full circle and I felt incredibly pleased with myself.

I was` Back from the Dead` The Phoenix has risen from the ashes.

Yes folks `Running has saved my life`

Having a passion for sport is a wonderful thing. It makes you feel good about yourself. It gives you challenges and goals to work towards. It keeps you motivated. But above all it gives you a reason to fight for the life you enjoy.

`Our way is not soft grass, it`s a mountain path with lots of rocks.
But it goes upwards, forwards toward the sun`

My hope in writing this book is to give Hope and Encouragement to others who are going through illness. Sometimes it is hard to see beyond the moment. However a year passes so quickly when you look back and you can set yourself goals to work towards. Take it one step at a time. Give yourself time to work towards your goal. I promise you it can be done. Don`t be hard on yourself. If you need a rest, take it and don`t beat yourself up. Learn to know your own body and treat it with the respect it deserves and it will repay you a hundred times over. I have done it so I know it can be done. Here are a few tips to help you:

- Take time for yourself. You deserve some `me time`.
- Try to eat healthily. This doesn't mean you have to forgo all treats. Treat yourself when you've reached one of your goals and then get working on your next goal.
- Running is not for everyone, but you can find an exercise you enjoy doing, find it and make it part of your daily routine and stick with it.
- Make sure you also get plenty of rest and relaxation.
- Surround yourself with positive people and avoid the energy drainers. They will do you no good at all.
- Get plenty of fresh air. It works wonders.
- Treat yourself to a regular massage. It really helps improve the lymph flow to detox the body.

It is a very rewarding feeling when you can take control of your own life and fight back from illness.

`If you believe
You can achieve`

I would like to leave you with a lovely quote

`Life may not be the party we`d hoped for
But while we`re here
We should Dance`

DANCE ON MY FRIENDS AND HEY!

REMEMEMBER YOUR INNER SMILE

In hospital I was on 9 different drugs. On release from hospital I was down to 7. I have gradually come off most of them. I now only take 2 which are Prednisolone the steroid which I am advised by Dr B to decrease each month down to zero. The other drug is my immunosuppressant Azathioprine. Who knows I may even get off that some time too, after all I`ve done it before.

My Muscle Measurement and Weight chart

	21st Dec 2011	14th Jan	14th Feb	Now. Oct 2012
Weight	8 stone	8st 3	8st 7	9stone
Waist	26inch	28	28	29
Thighs	18 inch	18 ½	19	21
Biceps	10inch	10	10	11
Calf	13 ½ inch	14	14	14
Hips	34inch	35	36	38

During those long weeks in hospital when I wasn't able to do anything my weight dropped dramatically and my muscles disappeared. However once the medication started to kick in and I was able to exercise I gradually got my well- toned body back to where it had been before. In fact, funnily enough I think I am now in even better shape than before as I was working harder than I ever had done before, and kept it up daily.
Before I went into hospital I had weighed 9 ½ stone. Since getting myself back up to fitness and health I have maintained a very healthy weight for me of 9 stone. I am also much more flexible. The first exercises I was able to do were simple stretches. I would do them daily as this was all I could manage. It has meant that when my muscles returned they were much more pliant and flexible. Always look for the Silver lining.
It was a lot of hard work and commitment to get myself back to fitness but hey it was well worth it. You too can do it. But I will warn you it is not easy, however `we all love a challenge`
Go to it my friends and I wish you all Health and Happiness. X

 The following pages are just some of the things that helped me on my way to recovery and I thought you might find helpful.

These are the Exercises I was given by the Physiotherapists at hospital. I was to start with only 10 repetitions. 10 were enough I can tell you, they were hard to do at first. I did them twice daily without fail. Once I found I had got stronger and was beginning to find these exercises a little bit easier I added in 10 more and then 10 more until I was doing 30 reps twice a day.

Along with all of these exercises of course I had my daily walk and I was doing a few minutes on my `Turbo` (my bike). The day Bob rigged it up for me I could only manage 3 minutes, however I persevered and I was slowly increasing the time I spent on it each day. I had the incentive of desperately wanting to get back on my bike proper and get outside.

I also had my mini- trampoline in the conservatory and I was at first just walking on it to try to improve my balance and strengthen my ankles and calves. After a few days I could manage a small bounce or two. I was like a kid in a sandpit. I cannot put into words how good it felt to be moving again. An added bonus of course was I had my lovely wee garden to look out to. My friend Julie(

STEP-UPS	YOGA BRIDGE	SQUATS
DROP KNEE BENDS	CAT STRETCH	WALL PRESS-UPS
HEEL RAISES	VERTICAL ARM RAISES With broom handle	SHOULDER PRESS With hand weight
LYING SIDE LEG LIFTS	BICEP CURLS With hand weight	TRICEP PULL-UPS With hand weight
LYING SIDE CLAMS	SIDE ARM RAISES With hand weight	WOBBLE BOARD

who is a gardener) had while I was in hospital come in and done all my window boxes at the front of my house and tidied all my back garden. It all looked fabulous.

Good Nutrition is also very important for all of us but for those fighting disease it is essential.

I truly believe 'You are what you eat' Over the years I have changed my diet for the better. My philosophy is

'If your Grandparents wouldn`t recognise it, Don`t eat it`

Let`s just think about that statement. They lived in a time where you didn't see anyone overweight let alone obese. I even remember when I was at school. (Yes, I know it's a long time ago) but there was one fat child in our whole school. One.

Our Grandparents would not have heard of additives and `E` numbers. Much of the food they ate was fresh, bought daily. They made everything as I might add did my mum. There were no convenience foods. The nearest thing to convenience food was milk being delivered to the door. There was no money for eating in between meals and you ate what you were given. This doesn't mean I don't have treats. Now and again I will have a bit of chocolate or a glass of wine, but it is `now and again` not every day or every week. I truly believe that healthy eating has played a major role in helping me fight these diseases. I try to take the 80/20 approach. 80% of the time I eat really healthily and 20% not quite so.

FOODS I AVOID

- Fizzy Drinks
- Anything with `E` numbers or additives
- Artificial sweeteners
- Convenience foods
- Cakes and Biscuits (I make my own healthy version)
- Crisps
- Sweets
- Meat
- Take Away food
- Pastry
- Bread

WHAT I EAT A LOT OF

- Fresh Fruit and Vegetables (particularly dark green veg)
- Peas, Beans and Lentils
- Sprouted Peas and Beans (I sprout these in jam jars on my window sill)
- Seeds: Pumpkin, Sesame, Sunflower, Chia, Hemp and Flax.
- Nuts (Unsalted mostly)
- Avocados
- Tahini
- Dried Seaweeds

- Ginger
- Oats
- Rice Cakes
- Rice
- Couscous
- Sweet Potatoes
- Turmeric powder
- Vanilla Soya Milk
- Almond Milk
- I also drink a lot of water, sometimes I add a drop of Organic Elderflower Cordial

WHAT I HAVE OCCASIONALLY
- Fish
- Eggs
- Dark Chocolate
- German white wine

Helpful websites

- www.lupusUK.co
- www.therawfoodscientist (Max my Vet friend)
- www.Myastheniagravis
- www.raynauds
- Juiceplus+
- sales@matoluk.com
- Facebook Lambert Eaton

Supplements I take are Matol Km. A herbal tonic consisting of the following:

- Chamomile Flower
- Thyme Leaf
- Angelica Root
- Passion Flower Herb
- Liquorice Root
- Polygala Sengala
- Saw Palmetto Berry
- Gentian Root
- Horsehound Herb
- Celery Seed
- Sarsaparilla Root
- Alfalfa Herb
- Dandelion Root

And JuicePlus+ . Vitamin and mineral powders made from 17 different fruits, vegetables and grains.

The last page is my exercise programme back to fitness. It starts the week I was released from the hospital. I am really pleased that I kept a record as it has been really interesting to look back and see the way I made progress by taking small steps. You too could do the same. Make a chart and keep a record of your achievements and don`t forget to give yourself a pat on the back for reaching those goals that you set yourself.

T

Dates	Walk(Miles)	Cycle(Miles)	Run(Miles)	Physic routine	Gym session
Week 1 26Dec-1 Jan	25	X	X	X 2 Daily	
Week 2 2 -8 Jan	29	X	X	X 2 Daily	
Week 3 9-15 Jan	21	12	X	X 2 Daily	
Week 4 16-22 Jan	22	22	X	X 2 Daily	
Week 5 23-29 Jan	19	35	X	X 2 Daily	
Week 6 30-5 Feb	18	27	1 ½ (My first run)	X 2 Daily	
Week 7 6-12 Feb	8 ½	20	1 ½	X 2 Daily	

I was back running and it felt so good.

Dates	Walk(Miles)	Cycle(Miles)	Run(Miles)	Physic routine	Gym session
Week 8 13-19 Feb	12	20	9	X 2 Daily	Did my 1st Friday Tai Chi and Falls class
Week 9 20-26 Feb	15	21	15	X 2 Daily	
Week 10 27-4 Mar	18	24	11	X 2 Daily	Did my 1st Monday Tai Chi class
Week 11 5-11 Mar	17	16	7	X 2 Daily	
Week 12 12-18Mar	13	In Devon Without my bike	12	X 2 Daily	
Week 13 19-25 Mar	12	32	15	X 2 Daily	Back to gym X 1
Week 14 26-1 Apr	12	24	26 1st official run – Jester fancy dress	X 2 Daily	X 2
Week 15 2-8 Apr	x	40	18	X 2 Daily	X 3
Week 16 9-15 Apr	x	32	26	X 2 Daily	X 2
Week 17 16-22 Apr	x	28	14	X 2 Daily	X 2
Week 18 23-29Apr	x	17	21	X 2 Daily	X 3

Dates	Walk(Miles)	Cycle(Miles)	Run(Miles)	Physic routine	Gym session
Week 19 30-6 May	x	21	20	X 2 Daily	X 1
Week 20 7-13 May	x	18	13	x 2 Daily	X 3
Week 21 14-20 May	34	X	17	X 2 Daily	X 3
Week 22 21-27 May	30	X	20 Edinburgh ½ Marathon	X Daily	X 1

The End

3443549R00056

Printed in Great Britain
by Amazon.co.uk, Ltd.,
Marston Gate.